The Yale Manuscript

Matthew Arnold ca. 1860

The Yale Manuscript

MATTHEW ARNOLD

Edited and with Commentary by
S. O. A. Ullmann

M.A.

THE UNIVERSITY OF MICHIGAN PRESS
Ann Arbor

1992   1991   1990   1989   4   3   2   1

Calligraphy by Abram Games.
Frontispiece courtesy of The Wordsworth Trust, Dove Cottage.
Yale Manuscript pages courtesy of the Yale University.

This book has been supported by a grant
from the National Endowment for the Humanities,
an independent federal agency.

Library of Congress Cataloging-in-Publication Data

Arnold, Matthew, 1822–1888.
  [Selections. 1988]
  The Yale manuscript / Matthew Arnold ; edited and with commentary
by S. O. A. Ullmann.
    p.   cm.
  A collection of documents, written by Matthew Arnold between 1843
and 1856/57, that contains poems, poetic fragments, and reflections
on life and art, held by the Beinecke Rare Book and Manuscript
Library of Yale University.
  Bibliography: p.
  Includes index.
  ISBN 0-472-10105-6 (alk. paper)
  1. Arnold, Matthew, 1822–1888—Notebooks, sketchbooks, etc.
I. Ullmann, S. O. A.   II. Beinecke Rare Book and Manuscript Library.
III. Title.
PR4021.U45 1989
828'.803—dc19   88-27669
                                                                        CIP

91-6138

Acknowledgments

This edition would not have been possible without the cooperation of many individuals who unselfishly gave of their time, knowledge, and manuscripts. My greatest debt is to Arnold Whitridge, Arnold's grandson, who permitted me to make copies of notebooks, poems, letters, and marginalia essential for dating and annotating the *YMS* and who also granted me permission to quote from these materials. Mrs. Mary Moorman patiently answered queries about her Arnold treasures. Roy McLaren, the former owner of a rich trove of Arnold manuscripts, now part of the Balliol collection, not only provided hospitality but allowed me to copy whatever I needed. The late Arthur Kyle Davis, Jr., showed me his vast microfilm collection of Arnold letters, and A. Dwight Culler sent me his copy of an invaluable inventory of Arnold's library.

Park Honan's hospitality, conversation, and correspondence could not help but contribute to my knowledge of Arnold. The late Kenneth Allott talked with me about the dating of poems and provided copies of manuscripts. Later Miriam Allott shared her enthusiasm for and understanding of Arnold with me. Regrettably, Douglas Bush, who provided inspiration and encouragement for many years, did not live to see the publication of this edition. He was an embodiment of the Arnoldian ideal.

R. H. Super provided many helpful suggestions. The value of his splendid edition of *The Complete Prose Works of Matthew Arnold* is attested to throughout this volume. Cecil Y. Lang, *the* modern editor of the letters of Victorian poets, saved me from a number of errors. Special thanks are due to Katharina Mommsen, who put her encyclopedic knowledge of Goethe at my disposal.

I have also benefited greatly from the suggestions of friends and colleagues who took the time to look over my manuscript: Frank Gado, who saw part of an early draft; Harry Marten, who read through a somewhat later one, and Harold C. Martin, retired from presidential labors, who skilfully red penciled my introduction. None, of course, are responsible for the weaknesses that remain. Other colleagues and former colleagues generously advised on sources and translations: Hans Freund, Peter Heinegg, Paul LeClerc, the late David Reece, William Thomas, and Anton Warde. Susan Ross helped to set up table 1.

Of the institutions that provided copies of manuscripts, obviously the most important is the Beinecke Rare Book and Manuscript Library of Yale University, which not only gave permission for the publication of the *YMS* (Tinker 21) and the reproduction of a number of its pages but also furthered my study of Arnold's handwriting with copies of the letters to Clough as well as of notebooks, poems, and other letters. Ms. Marjorie G. Wynne, recently retired Research Librarian, facilitated all this. She and her staff made working at the Beinecke a joy. I am grateful also to other libraries for providing copies of their Arnold manuscripts: the Balliol College Library (E. V. Quinn) and the Bodleian, Oxford; the Brotherton Library (David I. Masson and H. G. Tupper), the University of Leeds; the Dove Cottage Wordsworth archive (Stephen Gill); the British Library; the Lambeth Palace Library; and the Simmons College Library. Other libraries have kindly answered inquiries or provided facilities for research: the Widener Library, Harvard University; the New York Public Library and its Berg Collection; the Oriel College Library, Oxford; the University of California Library at Berkeley; and the Rush Rhees Library, the University of Rochester. I am especially grateful to the British Library at the British Museum, where much of the work on this edition was carried out. Its staff has been unfailingly courteous and helpful. The same, I am happy to add, can be said of the staff of the Schaffer Library, Union College.

I am grateful to the editors of the *Arnoldian* and of *Studies in Bibliography* for permission to make use of articles of mine.

Grants from the Union College Ford Faculty Development Fund provided assistance during the early stages of this project.

The University of Michigan Press wishes to acknowledge the support given toward the publication of this edition by the National Endowment for the Humanities.

Thanks also to an old friend, the distinguished artist Abram Games, who turned Arnold's initialed signature into the handsome design that graces the binding of this volume.

Finally, thanks to Thora Girke, one of the unsung heroines of academe, who efficiently took care of endless details.

Contents

Reproductions of Pages from the Yale Manuscript

Abbreviations and Symbols

Works by Matthew Arnold

CL — *The Letters of Matthew Arnold to Arthur Hugh Clough*. Edited by Howard Foster Lowry. London: Oxford University Press, 1932.

CPW — *The Complete Prose Works of Matthew Arnold*. Edited by R. H. Super. 11 vols. Ann Arbor: University of Michigan Press, 1960–77.

L — *Letters of Matthew Arnold, 1848–1888*. Edited by George W. E. Russell. London, 1895.

N-Bs — *The Note-Books of Matthew Arnold*. Edited by Howard Foster Lowry, Karl Young, and Waldo Hilary Dunn. London: Oxford University Press, 1952.

P — *The Poems of Matthew Arnold*. Edited by Kenneth and Miriam Allott. 2d ed. London: Longman, 1979.

UL — *Unpublished Letters of Matthew Arnold*. Edited by Arnold Whitridge. New Haven: Yale University Press, 1923.

YMS — "Yale Manuscript." Tinker 21. Beinecke Rare Book and Manuscript Library, Yale University.

Other Works

Allott, Reading-Lists" — Kenneth Allott. "Matthew Arnold's Reading-Lists in Three Early Diaries." *VS* 2 (1959): 254–66.

Barnes — Etienne Pivert de Senancour. *Obermann*. Translated by J. A. Barnes. 2 vols. London: Scott, 1910–15.

Commentary — C. B. Tinker and H. F. Lowry. *The Poetry of Matthew Arnold: A Commentary*. London: Oxford University Press, 1940.

Honan — *Matthew Arnold: A Life*. London: Weidenfeld; New York: McGraw-Hill, 1981.

Michaut — Etienne Pivert de Senancour. *Obermann*. Edited by Gustave Michaut. 2 vols. Paris: Hachette, 1912–13.

Spingarn — *Goethe's Literary Essays*. Edited by Joel E. Spingarn. New York: Harcourt, 1921.

Weigand	J. W. von Goethe. *Wisdom and Experience*. Selections by Ludwig Curtius. Translated and edited by Hermann J. Weigand. London: Routledge, 1949.
Werke	J. W. von Goethe. *Gedenkausgabe der Werke, Briefe, und Gespräche*. Edited by Ernst Beutler. 27 vols. Zurich: Artemis, 1948–71.
Werke [L.H.]	Goethe's *Werke*, Vollständige Ausgabe Letzer Hand. 60 vols. Stuttgart, 1827–42.

Periodicals

E & S	*Essays and Studies*
QR	*Quarterly Review*
RDM	*Revue des deux mondes*
SB	*Studies in Bibliography: Papers of the Bibliographical Society of the University of Virginia*
TLS	*Times Literary Supplement*
VS	*Victorian Studies*
YR	*Yale Review*

Symbols

°	substitutes for *sic* or indicates a corrected date
[ ]	brackets enclose editorial additions: page or entry numbers, dates, etc.

Introduction

Matthew Arnold's "Yale Manuscript" (*YMS*) includes poems and poetic fragments as well as hundreds of reflections on life and art, seminal ideas for many of his essays and most of his finest poems. C. B. Tinker and H. F. Lowry first described and named the collection in their *Commentary* (1940). Despite its title, it is not a single document but a sheaf of manuscripts: twenty-three miscellaneous sheets combined with fourteen sheets from a notebook, compiled and bound in leather after Arnold's death. Written between 1843 and 1856/57, the entries vary in length from a word to more than a page. Unlike his diaries and notebooks, which are filled with quotations, lists of appointments, and matters connected with Arnold's duties as a school inspector, most of the *YMS* consists of original material.

The *YMS* has been available for more than half a century, but because its entries are undated and its pages are not in chronological order, it has been impossible to make optimal use of its riches as a primary source of information about Arnold's intellectual and poetic development. Reliable dates for the entries in the *YMS* are essential if one wishes to understand the relationship between them and Arnold's first three volumes of poetry, published within five years: *The Strayed Reveller, and Other Poems* (1849), *Empedocles on Etna, and Other Poems* (1852), and *Poems* (1853). Fortunately, handwriting analysis makes it possible to date almost all the entries within a year. By arranging the manuscripts chronologically (based upon the date assigned to the earliest major entry on each page), this edition makes it possible to follow Arnold's development with relative ease. The apparently miscellaneous character of the entries has also limited the usefulness of the *YMS*. Their reordering and the cross-references in this edition reveal that most deal with a relatively small number of interrelated topics.

At no other period did Arnold produce notebook entries equal to the ones in the *YMS*. Some seem to speak even more directly to our time than do the comments in his published essays. There is much more coiled inside the entries than is at first apparent. Their suggestiveness stems in part from their unpolished state, and they are all the more resonant because Arnold does not attempt to spell out the connections among them. After all, Arnold was making these notes for his own benefit, not articulating an argument for the public. Free association accounts for more of the links between entries than does logic. Despite their relative lack of rhetorical distinction, they have a power stemming from Arnold's attempts to come to grips with such fundamental questions as the nature of knowledge; the place of man in the universe and in society; the function of language; and the role of reason, emotion, memory, and imagination, and their relationship to the totality of man's nature. In later years, after recognizing that satisfactory solutions to the enduring human problems were unlikely to be found, he turned his attention to less profound issues that could yield more tangible results. But for a few years, at least, Arnold was obsessed with trying to work out an "Idea of the world," as he called it, and, especially, an idea of the writer and of the man of action. Without these, Arnold believed, significant poetry could not be written, at least not by him. "Poets receive their distinctive character," he wrote much later, "not from their subject, but from their application to that subject of the ideas (to quote the *Excursion*) 'On God, on Nature, and on human life,' which they have acquired for themselves" (*CPW*, 1:210).

The title page is disingenuous, though not altogether untruthful (see p. 42). In 1843–44, while at Balliol College, Arnold did write two or three short poems on part of two pages of the notebook section of the *YMS*. The volume, however, does not contain any "notes on lectures." About 90 percent of the entries date, instead, from 1847–51 (and most from 1848–50), when he was serving in the undemanding post of private secretary to Lord Lansdowne, Lord President of the Council in Lord John Russell's Liberal cabinet.

Arnold usually spent much of his day on official duties and his evenings in an endless round of social gatherings, and yet he managed to find ample time for serious reading and reflection in an attempt to achieve self-knowledge and self-discipline.

These were also the years when he was writing most of his best poetry. Even the finest of the later poems—"Stanzas from the Grande Chartreuse," "The Scholar-Gipsy," "Thyrsis," and "Obermann Once More"—have their roots in the Lansdowne years.

The *YMS* includes some 345 lines of poetry: drafts of four published poems ("Written in Emerson's Essays," "Lines written in Kensington Gardens," "A Caution to Poets," and "The Second Best"); fragments of three others ("Tristram and Iseult," "Self-Deception," and "Empedocles on Etna"); seven poems he chose not to publish ("Rude Orator," "Sacrilege . . . ," "Night comes . . . ," "Man's Works," "The Pillars of the Universe," "To Meta," "And every man relates . . ."); and nine fragments of one to five lines each.[1]

In addition to his achievements as a poet during his Lansdowne years, Arnold made great strides intellectually and morally. Along with his letters to Arthur Clough, the *YMS* provides the earliest and fullest record of Arnold's struggle to find himself as a man and a writer. It reflects a new dedication to the life of the mind and a gradual commitment to writing as more than an agreeable pastime.

Taken as a whole, the *YMS* reflects Arnold's belated shift from years of intellectual passivity to activity. In making a commitment to writing, Arnold knew that he was not securing his financial future—that could wait until he was ready to marry—but he was showing that he was at last ready to abandon some of the pursuits that he had enjoyed as a youth and instead to concentrate on cultivating his literary gifts.

While much of Arnold's reading in the last half of his life was either practical (background for his essays) or meditative (sustenance for his spirit), in the Lansdowne years, as the *YMS* shows, it was exploratory—intended to help him understand the human condition, and, to a lesser extent, the nature of language, literature, and the role of the writer.

Goethe and Arnold's father are the major influences upon the

YMS. Arnold found in Goethe a mentor with whom he could usually agree about the human condition as well as about the nature and function of literature. In composing these entries, Arnold seems constantly to have had in mind Goethe's concerns and ideas, and sometimes even his words.[2] Dr. Arnold, on the other hand, is never mentioned or quoted, although his influence is nonetheless pervasive. In the *YMS* Matthew draws upon a number of writers to whom his father had introduced him: Guizot, Barante, and Bunsen (among others). Arnold's views sometimes directly reflect his father's. For example, both father and son were repelled and fascinated by Julius Caesar, noting his debauchery as well as his intellectual gifts and his genius as a leader. Dr. Arnold anticipated his son's assessment of Scott and the combination of admiration and skepticism with which he viewed Shakespeare. Dr. Arnold also introduced Matthew to Vico's cyclical view of history, which enabled both of them to see ancients as "modern" and relevant.

Arnold's literary and intellectual development began in earnest about the time that he started making entries in the *YMS*. The process by which he absorbed and transformed his reading into his own intellectual and moral being is sometimes readily apparent. For instance, from what Guizot had to say about Cromwell, Arnold gained insight into Julius Caesar, and through him he hoped to create an archetypal leader who could speak to Victorians about the nature of power and leadership (34r, p. 212). He usually selects a passage not because its ideas are new to him, but because it is a classical statement of an idea or attitude he already shares. His most important beliefs, moreover, usually have several sources that reinforce one another.

These entries indicate the course of his development and the way in which he prepared the ground for his published work. They were an integral part of the process that led to his maturing as a poet. As he devoted more time to the *YMS,* his poetry improved and became more abundant. Later, during the months immediately preceding his wedding and the early years of marriage and school inspecting, he no longer had time for systematic reading, reflection, and entries in the *YMS,* but he was able to compose a few fine poems and compile and publish two of his best volumes of poetry. Poetic composition did not fall off as abruptly as entries in the *YMS*, because he was able to tap reserves of thought and feeling stored up earlier. He added almost nothing to the *YMS* during his first five years as an inspector. Then, between March, 1856, and March, 1857, he produced a final page containing notes and ideas for "Lucretius," the tragedy he had been thinking about for a decade. Not long after, when he needed to prepare lectures as Professor of Poetry at Oxford, he began to read intensively once again and resumed note taking, but by then his focus had altered, and he did not return to the *YMS*.

In addition to encompassing Arnold's greatest burst of poetic creativity, the years 1847–51 marked the major turning point in his life. Before them lay the freedom of youth; after, the responsibilities of a husband and father and a job involving much travel and drudgery. In a letter to his sister Jane ("K") of January 25, 1851, he reflects sadly upon the passing of youth:

> The aimless and unsettled, but also open and liberal state of our youth we *must* perhaps all leave and take refuge in our morality and character; but with most of us it is a melancholy passage from which we emerge shorn of so many beams that we are almost tempted to quarrel with the law of nature which imposes it on us. (*L*)

Thoughts of man's self-made confusion and entanglement also occur in the letter, as they do in the sentence he quotes from Goethe on the first page of the *YMS:* "God has made man simple [unfragmented], but how he became wound up and entangled himself is difficult to say" (11[8], p. 57). About the same time, Arnold composed "The Second Best" and the observations that follow it in the *YMS* (pp. 194–95). All reflect his state of mind. Line 10, in particular— "Human things so fast entangled"—picks up Goethe's image. The "hopeless tangle of our age" ("Stanzas in Memory of the Author of 'Obermann'," line 83) may also echo Goethe. "Empedocles on Etna," I.ii.204–5 expresses the same idea but uses a different image. All suggest the inevitable loss of vision and the limiting of options that come with the passing years.

5

"Nothing makes me more despise the world," he complains amid the political bustle of Lansdowne House, "than the homage it pays to experience." The "ease" of the man of the world does not come from a noble soul or a philosophic mind, "but it generally implies only the total absence of all youth & richness of soul, and the presence of a dead barren negative callosity," leading to "suffocation" (5v[3], p. 168). Arnold's attempt to retain his youth was an attempt to remain uncommitted, sensitive, vital, and creative.

But his productive and pivotal Lansdowne years were also among the most emotionally stressful of his life. In the months immediately preceding his marriage, he noted in his diary that he was wracked by headaches, toothaches, and other aches and pains. He was in love, but he was also frequently depressed. It may seem surprising that he accomplished so much, given the strain under which he was working, but the emotional ferment helped to deepen his poetry, and the troughs of depression seem to have been offset by mildly manic highs.

Even at the time, Arnold sensed that one period of his life was ending. He yearned for a way to live that would allow him to develop all facets of his being but feared that finding a way to earn enough to support a family would probably mean abandoning cherished parts of himself. For a while he had been able to combine politics with poetry, but he knew he would soon have to choose between them, between a life of commitment and one of detachment. Entries commenting on the man of action and on the poet-artist point to the terms of the choice. The freedom of spirit and contemplative solitude of the poet's life appealed to Arnold, but his family heritage and the times demanded a life of commitment and service to humanity.

He admitted to "K" that "the worldly element" entered into him more than into her (L, January 25, 1851), but that side of him— his gregariousness, his banter, his love of life and of fine clothes, and his passion for sports—has no place in these jottings. Rather, it is his introspective side that is uppermost. Because these pages were primarily meant to assist him as a writer who saw himself in the classical tradition, he limits himself to what he feels to be the enduring concerns of man.

The possibility of a career combining commitment and detachment had long tantalized him. Even in his first published poem, "Alaric at Rome," he had stressed the conqueror's detachment. The poem describes not the heat of battle but a moment of calm, when Alaric stands apart on a hill and reflects on his conquest. The same outlook pervades Arnold's Newdigate Prize poem, "Cromwell" (1843). Likewise, on the last page of the *YMS* (34r[3], p. 212), written after Arnold had decided upon a career as school inspector and had chosen to marry within the Establishment, he portrays Caesar and Cromwell as remarkably aloof men of action; or rather, selects a period of relative detachment in their careers. He focuses on the independence of these leaders and their ability to improvise, qualities shared with poets. More and more, he became convinced that the artist and the activist need not lead antithetical lives. Yet in the *YMS* he notes how rare it is for any man to find expression for all sides of himself. For this reason, success should be measured not in terms of money or fame but of self-realization.

Arnold's projected drama "Lucretius" probably would have stressed not only the struggle between the Milonians and Clodians but also the more fascinating contrast between the inadequate Epicurean poet Lucretius and the extraordinary man of action Julius Caesar. Through their contrasting goals and ideals and their attitudes toward success and failure, freedom and determinism, life and death, Arnold hoped to explore the implications of both the contemplative and the active life.

In moments of depression he doubted that wisdom was to be achieved through either art or action:

The Spirit of *Life* pours itself into this or that man, & the power and vivacity of his operations make the feeble ghostlike mass of mankind adore him, & follow his oracles as if the Spirit of *Truth* had dictated them: but it is not so: Caesar, Goethe, Napoleon are mightily enstrengthened by the indwelling Spirit of *Life:* but the Spirit of *Truth* incarnates itself seldom or never in man. If ever, in the still & hardly known. (9r[3], p. 186)

This is a puzzling entry because it seems to discredit not only Caesar and Napoleon but even Wordsworth (later replaced by Caesar) and Goethe, whom Arnold regarded as the supreme modern sage. Arnold does not even distinguish here between men of action and men of letters. He attributes most of men's achievements, and the ensuing public acclaim, not to their vision of the Truth, but to their vitality and charisma. Neither deeds nor words are adequate to express the Spirit of Truth, which transcends both. Active participation in life, even utterance itself—expression, "publicity"—gets in the way of Truth (see 6r[2], p. 171).

With Arnold's appointment as private secretary to Lord Lansdowne came more direct involvement with political issues and politicians. In 1848, Continental revolutions and the repressive reactions they triggered as well as Chartist agitations at home gave political, economic, and social questions additional urgency. In that year, comments on such matters become more numerous in the *YMS*, anticipating by nearly two decades ideas he treated at length in *Friendship's Garland* and *Culture and Anarchy*.

In the *YMS*, he observes:

—The common run of men have no special gift & can be applied to anything—All work is for them merely occupation. Stupid Hobbs who digs turnips would be stupid still if he had Lord Dulls° library to read in, and leisure to think in: and so the world loses nothing by his remaining where he is. And genius is seldom left digging in a turnip field without being acknowledged: it has the more chance of being acknowledged from their° being a large idle and rich class to be amused by it and to protect it. So under an aristocracy with all its apparent inequalities, a nation gets perhaps all the benefit that is to be got out of its members. (24r^1–v^1, p. 75)

Arnold never became a democrat, but experience with countless schools for the poor later made him much more sympathetic toward "the common run of men." In preferring "central offical Govt." to "local *class* Govt.," he recognizes, like J. S. Mill *On Liberty* more than a decade later, that the former "does not develope the capacity & self respect of local populations" (24r[1], p. 75).

From an apparently disinterested point of view, he here considers what is best for the nation. Yet his comments on "apparent inequalities" fail to concede, even if one accepts his argument that under aristocratic government the loss of talent to the state is negligible, that the inequalities remain and are substantial. Stupid Hobbs might prefer Lord Dull's leisure to a life of turnip digging, even were he to share the nobleman's stupidity or "the Barbarian's imperviousness to ideas," as Arnold would later have put it (cf. "Horatian Echo," stanza 2).

The reference to Hobbs and Lord Dull shows that Arnold almost instinctively turned to the creation of character to embody social attitudes.

The following entry continues his reflections on class and government:

—This is what may be said to show people that the present state of things is one under which no harm or loss befalls: but the great argument is that it is inevitable. Take your crust & be thankful—for if the social fabric be shaken you will lose even that. . . . this menace does in fact do much to frighten and make them plod on as they are. How many mothers & wives preach throughout England everyday: the duty of not endangering this crust. What potent auxiliaries are these to the cause of what is called social order.—Take care, then, governments that every one has his crust. (24v[1]–r[2], pp. 75–76)

Arnold usually comments forthrightly on aesthetic, ethical, and religious issues, but he seems unwilling here to speak directly on the issue of class. Instead, he makes use of oblique rhetorical strategies to deal with it. His views appear remarkably reactionary when stated baldly without ironic persiflage. For those potentially explosive times, Arnold seems to be endorsing an arrangement based upon fear: the poor settle for the status quo because of fear of starvation, while the government ensures subsistence out of fear of revolution.

These comments reflect young Arnold's basic sympathy for the aristocracy, unlike his father who loathed it. On the whole, Arnold treats the Barbarians more gently than the other two classes and rather regrets the aristocracy's inevitable passing as a source of stability: "man is born with a 'turn for being a sovereign prince,' " he confides, "& accordingly this desire, as all his, is stereotyped in the actual & visible world by the existence of aristocracies &c—to be sure the individual desirer is often not one of them—but the rule is saved— let that content him!" (36r[1], p. 98).

Arnold had been reading Burke, whom he greatly admired, but his defense of aristocracy is more psychological than Burke's. Given the hysteria then gripping England, Arnold's idea that institutions are not so much eternal verities as stereotypes designed to embody and satisfy basic human wishes is part of a surprisingly sophisticated and disinterested vision of human society.

. In a rare early thrust at aristocracies Arnold comments: "Even aristocracies putting in force social tyrannies avoid appearing to act directly for & from themselves, but put forward the law as an awful necessity behind them & their victims equally" (37r[1][3], p. 83). Arnold is surprisingly blunt in his references to "social tyrannies" and "victims," and in his attack on the hypocrisy of hiding behind necessity and (natural) law. Lansdowne's secretary must have observed much that contributed to this disillusioned view of political manipulation.

As the letters to Clough written at this time also indicate, Arnold distrusted the ignorant masses in England and yet found no guiding wisdom in the aristocracy. Any action taken by the masses, he assumed, would be hasty, mistaken, and self-serving.

Political solutions may at best help the herd, but for "the Spiritual," "mending" is needed (33r[3], 22r, pp. 139, 79). It involves self-improvement and self-control rather than rights and privileges. Arnold's emphasis upon being rather than doing anticipates his vision of culture as "*a study of perfection*": "an *inward* condition of the mind and spirit . . . at variance with the mechanical and material civilisation in esteem with us . . ." (*CPW*, 5:91, 95). What his later formulation adds is that the pursuit of perfection requires one to "carry others along with him" (*CPW*, 5:94).

In the *YMS* Arnold is testing attitudes and ideas, anatomizing himself and his age, and searching for their counterparts in other times and places. Underlying all else is determinism, his belief that he is living in a universe whose laws "are irrespective of man" (32r[1], p. 89).[3] In a world where cause and effect operate impartially, without pity or compromise, man ought "not to *abuse* or *storm at* the Gods or Fate," for "nothing [is] wilfully operating against us" (32v[4], 33r[1], pp. 89, 139). True freedom can be attained only by Stoically learning what nature demands and then using one's will to serve her.[4] Arnold's Empedocles shares Spinoza's belief that man must submit to nature and act in accordance with her laws: "To tunes we did not call our being must keep chime" (I.ii.196).

Related to his determinism was his belief in the influence of one's age. Looking back on these years, Arnold wrote to Arthur Clough: "woe was upon me if I analysed not my situation: & Werter Réné° & such like none of them analyse the modern situation in its true *blankness* and *barrenness,* and *unpoetrylessness*" (from MS; *CL,* 126). The implications of this assertion are central to understanding the *YMS.* Arnold equates his "situation" with "the modern situation" in the belief that one's era largely determines the possibilities for one's life. In comparing himself with Goethe's Werther and Châteaubriand's René, he fuses the fictive and the autobiographical.

Arnold's attempt to understand his age and, through it, himself is the thread that connects many of the apparently heterogeneous entries in these manuscripts. The search for understanding was essential both for the sake of his mental health and his writing.

One of the major questions he confronted was the extent to which people can alter the major forces of their age. In time he came to share the view expressed by Goethe in a letter to Schiller of July 21, 1798: "Your own epoch you cannot change. You can, however, oppose its trend and lay the groundwork for auspicious developments" (Weigand, 175; *Werke,* 20:602).[5] On the one hand, Arnold was convinced that man's thoughts, feelings, and beliefs are largely determined by his age. (As he notes in the *YMS:* "The Spirit of the world enounces the problems which this or that generation of men is to work . . . . Those who attempt to enounce & work their own have the fate of all intempestive things—they perish" (9v–10r[4], p. 189). On the other hand, even if the river of time cannot be compelled to reverse its direction and the cycles of history cannot be altered, man can try to mitigate the worst features of his age.

Most of Arnold's reading supported these assumptions. For example, in 1845, he reread Barante's *Tableau de la littérature française pendant le dix-huitième siècle* (1813), to which he had been introduced by his father in the sixth form at Rugby (Allott, "Reading-Lists," 259; Stanley [1844], 2:49). In his opening paragraphs, Barante stresses literary determinism. Our times shape "our style, our conceits, our habitual impressions" (3). He even uses Arnold's favorite water imagery to portray the time-stream, although he does not call it that: "the direction in which writers travelled was marked out to them by the age. It was a current which they navigated; their movements hastened its rapidity, but the age gave it the first impulse" [1833], 6; [1813], 7).

A clue to much of Arnold's thinking in the *YMS* lies in his attitude toward the past. Following the ancients and indirectly Vico, he viewed history as cyclical, but usually collapsed the traditional four ages into two: golden ages that are innocent, religious, and unified; and modern or iron ages that are complex, rational, skeptical, neurotic, and fragmented. By studying other modern ages, he hoped to avoid their mistakes and learn how to preserve the remnants of those capacities possessed by healthier, undivided ages before the fall into reason. It became second nature for Arnold to think of himself in Roman terms. As he wrote to Clough, "we deteriorate in spite of our struggles—like a gifted Roman falling on the uninvigorating atmosphere of the decline of the Empire" (*CL,* 123, Jan.° 7, 1852).[6] Out of Arnold's study of history came not only a degree of self-knowledge but also poetry, his chief means of exploring aspects of himself under a wide variety of conditions.

Arnold tended to interpret historical epochs in psychological terms.

In the following comment, he brings together some of his most deeply rooted convictions about man and history:

> Why are we so interested in origines°, and in the dark ages[?] Because man had in one case not overexcited himself—& in the other had succeeded in forgetting—had thrown off the burden of his over-stimulated, sophisticated, artificialized false-developed miserable nervous sceptical self, and begun life anew. To this the race when over-cultivated tends, and does now tend, & did tend in the Roman times. (7v[3]–8r, p. 199)

The earliest ages combine faith with imagination and possess a unified sensibility. The dark ages avoid the maladies of modern ages by regressing. This dichotomy owes much to romantic primitivism, with its search for cultural origins and its interest in "innocence," whether in child, peasant, gypsy, or simpleton.
Elsewhere in the *YMS* he writes:

> The Roman world perished for having disobeyed reason and nature.
> The infancy of the world was renewed with all its sweet illusions[.]
> [B]ut infancy and its illusions must for ever be transitory, and we are again in the place of the Roman world . . . .
> O let us beware how we again are false to [right reason and nature] . . . ." (35r[1], p. 160)

This entry reveals an apparent contradiction in Arnold's cyclical view of history. When the final stage (modernity) has been reached, it must inevitably be succeeded by the start of a new cycle (infancy). Yet Arnold blames the return to infancy upon the failure to obey "reason and nature," as if men could prevent the inevitable return to the beginning that is built into the cyclical theory. Presumably, what he wants, despite his nostalgia for youth and the youthful world, is a prolongation of the final phase.
His early poems and letters are filled with references to the contrast

between his own "unpoetical" and "damned times," and the pastoral calm and wholeness of ancient Greece or the heyday of Christianity. Yet his attitude toward "modern" ages was deeply ambivalent. He was fascinated by the "modern" Rome of Cicero and Augustus, considering it in 1857 "perhaps, on the whole, the greatest, the fullest, the most significant period on record," despite the fact that it had failed to produce an adequate literature (*CPW*, 1:32). But he also believed that

> [t]he predominance of thought, of reflection, in modern epochs is not without its penalties; in the unsound, in the over-tasked, in the over-sensitive, it has produced the most painful, the most lamentable results; it has produced a state of feeling unknown to less enlightened but perhaps healthier epochs—the feeling of depression, the feeling of *ennui*. (*CPW*, 1:32)

Two contemporary entries (17r, 2r, pp. 142, 145) illustrate the close links between Arnold's analysis of his "diseased" age and himself. One focuses on "spiritual distress"; the other, on "the misery of the present age." The former stresses the need to observe "the movement of the world," to be aware of one's place in the historical cycle, if one is to avoid taking "the wrong step." The consequences of a misstep are "confusion,"[7] or, as Arnold at first revealingly wrote, "misery." The word *misery* seems too acutely personal for a generalization about man's relation to major movements of thought and belief. "Misery," however, accurately describes Arnold's state of mind at the time and his largely fruitless attempt to overcome "spiritual distress." Although Arnold's diaries for 1849–50 have not survived, his 1851 diary typically records early in the year: "could never collect myself," "wretched nervous day," "unsettled," "uneasy," "uncomfortable."

Arnold's attempt to overcome "spiritual distress" by achieving "mastery over [him]self & the world" is a major theme of the *YMS*. It accounts for his reflections on the nature of God, on the subterranean self, on cause and effect, and on limitations and necessity. By 1853, realizing how many had lost their sense of direction, Arnold dubbed the epoch itself "an age of spiritual discomfort," that is, an age that provided no relief for those suffering from spiritual distress (*CPW*, 1:14).

Arnold planned to devote large-scale works not to those whom he admired for triumphing over spiritual distress—Sophocles, Shakespeare, and Goethe—but to those whose "unsuccessful" attempts at self-mastery he could empathize with: Lucretius and Empedocles.

On the other hand, the use of the word *misery* to describe "the present age" is appropriate, for here he is really commenting upon the misery of modern man, again connecting psychology and history. It is likely that he unconsciously took as his starting point Carlyle's essay "Characteristics" (1831). In commenting upon "the misery which has fallen on man in our Era," Carlyle attributes the cause largely to our diseased consciousness, akin to what Arnold later called the "dialogue of the mind with itself" (*Works*, 28:29; cf. the quotation by Henry Taylor given on p. 17 following). Doubtless using introspection as his chief investigative tool, Arnold begins by describing man's lack of feeling, or at least the shallowness of his feelings, and then notes its probable cause: the torrent of transitory stimuli pulling us in many directions. The root of the misery, however, is alienation ("divorce from oneself"), paradoxically combined with self-consciousness. What one is probably conscious of is an inability to make contact with one's real, central, or buried self. "[O]ur remotest self," he notes, "must abide in its remoteness awful & unchanged, presiding at the tumult of the rest of our being, changing thoughts contending desires &c as the moon over the agitations of the Sea" (9r[1], p. 186). Here the self is the still point of our turning world. The aimless flux of human existence, described so movingly on sheet 2r (p. 145), is subject to human control, even though that control is remote and "must abide in its remoteness." In addition, our "real central life is something exquisitely kind, fine tempered, liberal, in good taste, unenvious[,] comfortable in itself" (6v[3]–7r, p. 178). Elsewhere, however, Arnold observes that dissatisfaction with our inner condition tempts us to seek to escape into the world without us, but in vain, for "every man's self is an unshakeoffable poor-relation whom he may go into no new sphere without taking with him" (9v[1], p. 189).[8] The apparent contradictions result from the fact that Arnold is already distinguishing between what he was later to call our ordinary self and our best or ideal self; the former "unshakeoffable," the latter remote and usually inaccessible.

The cost of modernity weighed heavily upon him, especially in these early years. His sense of being "hurl'd" into a hostile environment surfaces in "A Farewell," lines 85–86; "Stanzas written in Kensington Gardens," line 25; "Destiny," line 7; and others.[9] He tried, literally and symbolically, withdrawing to the mountains, visiting a monastery, and, most tempting of all, seeking seclusion in glades, but ultimately he recognized all these as escapes that leave man limited and maimed. His ideal was to live in the modern world without becoming contaminated by it. For a Victorian, mastery over self and the world seemed the only appropriate alternative to spiritual distress. But since Arnold found that neither form of mastery was attainable, except to a very limited extent, the distress lingered on until marriage and school inspecting took him out of himself and away from his life as a poet.

Nineteenth-century self-consciousness combined with revulsion from what he considered a sick society made Arnold turn inward for renewal. As he remarks in the *YMS*, "you must plunge yourself down to the depths of the sea of intuition: all other men are trying as far as lies in them to keep you on the barren surface" (8r[1], p. 203). Again Arnold shows his awareness of the importance of the nonrational, not only as a source of inspiration but also as a force in our daily lives.

Madness also fascinated him. He saw it as a disease that afflicts societies as well as individuals. In poems written during this period, he more than once describes humanity as raving ("A Farewell," line 87; "Lines written in Kensington Gardens," line 26); and his Goethe in "Memorial Verses" looks down upon a world of "insane distress," line 31). The Victorians, we need to recall, regarded as mad much that we simply consider neurotic. For Arnold, madness also included some of Bacon's "idols" or fallacies of the mind.

On the first sheet of the *YMS*, spanning the years from 1843 to 1850/51, Arnold links the names of Stephens, De Vere, Planche, and Barbier with the comment "pride is madness" (1r[4–7], p. 57).

The types of madness that particularly interest him here are mono-mania, presumption, and morbid self-consciousness.

Gustave Planche's review of August Barbier's poem on England, *Lazare,* and in particular the section entitled "Bedlam," provided Arnold with a ready-made symbol for much that he deplored in himself and in his age. Barbier's London seems to anticipate Gustave Doré's vision of an infernal city and T. S. Eliot's godless wasteland. Bedlam is no longer primarily an institution for the insane or for raving social misfits but the inevitable destination of modern man.[10]

In the life and work of George Stephens, Arnold found a perfect example of monomania (see p. 59). No amount of derision directed at Stephens's bombastic pseudo-Jacobean plays on stage or in print could shake his faith in them. With egregious zeal, he even wrote plays that focused on his own mania, such as *Self-Glorification: A Chinese Play for the Times.* Its protagonist, Chu, is a poet whose "wits are tainted, cracked with overweening" (Stephens, *Dramas for the Stage,* 2:119).[11]

Beneath the name of Stephens, Arnold added Aubrey De Vere's surname. Henry Taylor's anonymous review of *The Waldenses* in the *Quarterly Review* summarizes the career of the protagonist of "A Tale of the Modern Time": "a devout and happy childhood, a daring and presumptuous youth, a manhood inebriated with intellectual power and pride . . . [leading to] self-abhorrence symbolized in the persecution of a man by a phantom of himself . . ." (*QR* 72 [1843]: 158). The poem, says Taylor, warns against the modern intellectual whose mind turns inward for lack of activity. Arnold's Empedocles embodies many of the traits that Taylor attributes to De Vere's protagonist. In his preface to *Poems* (1853), Arnold also attacks the mad pride, the "delirium of vanity," of poets who think it their mission to praise modern society (*CPW*, 1:13).

"Tristram and Iseult," III.112–50, omitted from the 1853 and 1854 editions of the poem, takes on added significance when viewed as a tirade not simply against passion but against madness as well. The speaker singles out the monomaniacal ambition of Caesar and Alexander, characterizing it as unnatural and possessed by "a diseased unrest" (an almost redundant epithet).[12]

Arnold attempted to deal with madness by probing its deep roots in his age, in man's nature, and, especially, in the artist. For some years to come the idea of madness, broadly interpreted, continued to concern him. "Sanity,—that is the great virtue of the ancient litera-ture; the want of that is the great defect of the modern . . . ." The absence of sanity also gives rise to "caprice and eccentricity" (*CPW*, 1:17). This foreshadows Arnold's essay on "The Literary Influence of Academies," with its attack on English eccentricity and lack of urbanity.

Another key concept in the *YMS* is "affinity." It tells us much about Arnold's view of man's connections with his world. "[W]e can only *remember*," he notes, "what had *affinity to us*" (15r[3], p. 100), that is, what borders upon us, something largely determined by our location in time and place. If knowledge is memory, then knowledge, too, depends upon the chance experiences that control memory (31r[1], p. 109).[13]

Arnold's interest in affinity in the *YMS*, as well as slightly later in "A Farewell," was probably stimulated by reading Goethe's *Die Wahl-verwandtschaften (Elective Affinities)*. The plot involves the separation and joining in a different combination of two couples. "Affinities really become interesting," says the husband, "only when they bring about separations" (40; *Werke,* 9:42).[14] Arnold's "Switzerland" poems are in part a study of the operation of affinity or, more precisely, of an affair doomed because of lack of affinity.

The first entry on sheet 21r[1] (p. 102) links affinity with the idea of "correspondence" and exposes some of the basic differences that separate Arnold from his predecessors, the English romantic poets. For them the connection between man and nature, thought and thing, was still intimate, despite the Cartesian and scientific revolutions that had led philosophers and scientists to reject analogical thinking as a mode of discovering truth. For Arnold, on the other hand, the split between man and the external world was a fundamental fact of ex-perience. He yearned for unity and wholeness, but he experienced separateness and isolation (cf. "Empedocles on Etna," II.352–54). Where the romantics speak of fusion and harmonies, Arnold's dual-ism leads him to think in terms of juxtaposition and fixities, what

Coleridge would have denigrated as an operation of the fancy rather than the imagination. Yet although Arnold no longer takes correspondence for granted, when he actually observes it, he finds it comforting and life enhancing.

Arnold conceived of existence as divided into two "provinces" ("the natural & spiritual world") and two "operations" that express the functioning of each. He tried to construct a universe empirically and inductively upon this dualistic framework. Relying upon observation and "facts," he rejected deductions based upon the consoling principle of universal analogy and correspondence that, at least since the Middle Ages, had assumed a relationship between the two worlds. Because that principle seemed to him to have no basis either in reason or in experience, he imagined that acceptance of analogies must have originated in an authority that "order[s] us to infer likeness" (21v[1][1], p. 102). Correspondences are pleasurable, Arnold admits, but they must be supported by empirical observation. When so supported, and only then, do they help to validate the inner life and make experience more memorable, thus helping to overcome alienation from self. The inner self is feeble, but correspondence or contact with the external world gives it renewed vitality, much as contact with the earth revived Antaeus.[15]

Opposition to the fragmentariness and lack of direction of human existence figures prominently in the *YMS* and in Arnold's poetry. "What a thing it is to have a reason in oneself for doing or not doing a thing and how few have experienced it," he laments (11r[1], p. 180). The "reason in oneself" is something to be "experienced" rather than arrived at by some elaborate chain of reasoning. Arnold has in mind acting in accordance with right reason and one's real, buried self, from which modern man is usually alienated. As he explained to Clough, my "one natural craving is not for profound thoughts, mighty spiritual workings &c &c but a distinct seeing of my way as far as my own nature is concerned . . ." (*CL*, 110; see also *CL*, 85).[16] This involved being able to give expression to his true self: "To desire to be *natural* in conversation, & not to have the *force* necessary to supply the demands this desire makes on your collectedness invention &

spirit" (9r[4], p. 186). Naturalness is difficult to achieve. Because finding our own style is not easy, our behavior and utterances tend to be imitative. Arnold's failure in his own eyes made him aware of his lack of force. Several comments from about the same time stress the curse of weakness: "to be weak is to be miserable" (*Commentary*, 293, echoing *Paradise Lost*, 1:157; see also "Lucretius," fragment iv [*P*, 649], "A Farewell," lines 21ff., and "Courage," which links weakness with lack of steadfastness: "Our bane, disguise it as we may, / Is weakness, is a faltering course" [lines 25–26]).

In his earliest published letter to Clough (1845), he asks: "have you a great Force of Character? That is the true Question. For me, I am a reed, a very whoreson Bullrush . . ." (*CL*, 56). In the very act of admitting his lack of force, he falls into a mock-Elizabethan mode, thus illustrating how difficult he found it to be natural. Arnold seems to be trying to act out and express his deepest and truest self directly, rather than through role playing, but for the moment it takes more force than he can muster consistently. He discovers, in true Stoical fashion, that naturalness is the result of self-mastery, not of spontaneously following the inclinations of the moment or "Doing As One Likes."

Although Arnold was "the Emperor" to his younger sisters and brothers and was much in demand at London dinner parties, he was aware that his behavior was far from perfection. Hence his lifelong search for profound inwardness, calm steadiness, and moral stability. Even when he notes a gaily attired Cockney on a steamer, it is to turn back upon himself and wonder about the ultimate figure he is cutting in the world, not simply his own elegant facade but his actual success in dealing with the fundamental problems of life and human relationships (37v^1–r^2[6], pp. 83–84). Most of the time he tries to universalize his experience and make it available for poetry. The lover of Marguerite, the weary Empedocles, the dying Tristram, all suffer from forms of unease, restlessness, and spiritual distress commented upon in these pages. Arnold notes the necessity, on the one hand, of bowing to the conditions of existence; on the other, of pursuing perfection.

One of the main sources that Arnold explored in his search for self-discipline was oriental religious philosophy and particularly the Bhagavad Gita:

> By meditation & observation we attain a faith, & strike one day some good strokes in manners & behaviour: ha, say we, what a power conviction lends to our practice: the next day the nerves are wrong, the manners full of blunder & despicabilitiy, and the conviction, metamorphosed into consciousness, riding us like a nightmare. Nor is it true that after repeated failures, we stand. ($37r^2[7]$, p. 84)

Arnold's interest in religion at this time stemmed primarily from its impact on practice: manners, behavior, or what, in his prose works, he calls "conduct." He is disillusioned when his new faith fails to work. Under the influence of "nerves," conviction gives way to debilitating (self-)consciousness, and achievement, to nightmare.

Few comments reveal so much as these about Arnold's struggle toward calm and balance, or reveal how much anguish lay behind his ultimate achievement of self-control. The contrast between "some good strokes in manners & behaviour" and "manners full of blunder & despicability" goes far beyond pointing to some slight increase in awkwardness. The use of the word *metamorphosed* to describe the change from "conviction" to "consciousness" suggests that from one day to the next, inexplicably, he feels and acts like a different person. Despite his reading, reflection, and effort to achieve a calm and detached Stoic faith, he cannot maintain the self-control he longs for. Even more, he reveals how often he felt an enigma to himself, unable fully to communicate with himself, tap his powers, or guide his own thoughts and feelings. He recognizes the mysteriousness within his own being of the "daemonic" and constantly strives to understand and come to grips with it. Out of this struggle came some of his most moving poems.

Arnold soon gave up the Bhagavad Gita, but he did not cease to seek support from other sources. The quotations in his annual diaries testify to his continuing search for faith to reinforce conduct. Again and again he returns to favorite passages. They apparently needed constant renewal if they were to retain their talismanic influence.

Some time between August, 1849, and August, 1850, Arnold noted:

> —I cannot conceal from myself the objection which really wounds & perplexes me from the religious side is that the service of reason is freezing to feeling, chilling to the religious mood.
>
> & feeling & the religious mood are eternally the deepest being of man, the ground of all joy & greatness for him. (35r[2], p. 160)

This entry is the earliest and fullest sympathetic comment on religion in these pages. It should be seen in the context of his note on "spiritual distress," which insists on the error of returning to "fervent religion" at the modern stage in the historical cycle (17r, p. 142). Even here, however, when supporting the religious side of the argument, his interest lies in the utility of "the religious mood" rather than in religious belief. For some years, in fact, religion mattered to Arnold less as a system of belief than as something that brought emotional warmth and consolation.

Lionel Trilling claimed that central to most of Arnold's criticism "is the reconciliation of the two traditions whose warfare had so disturbed his youth—rationalism and faith" (*Matthew Arnold*, 177). The two entries on 35r (p. 160) support and make explicit the terms of that warfare and also provide an excellent example of Arnold's dialectical method. He presents two apparently incompatible truths, and then devotes himself in poetry and prose to trying to achieve some synthesis like "imaginative reason" or "morality touched with emotion," a faith without dogma or at least without illusions.

Several entries reflect Arnold's interest in non-Christian conceptions of God. One note, much indebted to Spinoza (23r, p. 192), points in the direction of Arnold's late definition of deity as *"the stream of tendency by which all things seek to fulfil the law of their being"* (*CPW*, 7:202 and elsewhere; for other views of deity, see 19v[1][2–3] and 5r[1], pp. 106 and 165). Yet in another entry Arnold attacks Spinoza for an uncharacteristic passage that shows traces of medieval scholasticism (10r[5], p. 189). After all, what had attracted Arnold to Spinoza was the fact that for him God was something to be experienced rather than derived from proofs. Many years later Arnold was still insisting that the idea of God in the Bible does not depend "on a metaphysical conception of the necessity of certain deductions from our ideas of cause, existence, identity, and the like; but on a moral perception of a rule of conduct not of our own making . . ." (*Literature and Dogma* [1873], *CPW*, 6:242).

On the final sheet of entries, 34r[5] (p. 212), he notes Caesar's lack of *Halt,* a German word that epitomizes one of Arnold's most important ideals. For all Caesar's genius, Arnold found him deficient in this essential moral (and aesthetic) quality. Much later, in reviewing the third volume of Curtius' *History of Greece,* he provided his fullest gloss on this key term:

> what differentiates Ionian Athens from Asiatic Ionia, is the gravity, the steadiness, the centripetal influence tending to a common Hellenism, to religious fixity, and to conservative habits. . . . This steadiness, or *Halt,* as Goethe calls it, for a long time balanced in the Athenians their native vivacity and mobility." (*CPW,* 5:274)

Arnold seems to have felt the necessity of *Halt* to balance his own "native vivacity." Behind the numerous images of restlessness, wavering, and wandering in his poetry, lies the search for *Halt.*

His encomium upon Sophocles as one "who saw life steadily, and saw it whole" ("To a Friend," line 12) combines two of Arnold's major concerns: *Halt* and wholeness. To respond to the whole when most people are fragmented and confined to what has affinity to them is as great an achievement as remaining steady when all is in flux.

Arnold saw in himself a reflection of the restlessness, turbulence, and lack of wholeness of his age. By the late 1840s he was struggling to achieve *Halt* for himself and later for his times as well, the equiv-
an "ever-fixèd mark" in a world of mutability. Despite the "confused multitudinousness" he saw around him in life and art, he continued to believe in an ideal that comprehended the classical values of unity, harmony, order, and singleness of purpose.

Goethe, in his autobiography, quotes Hamann to the effect that "everything that man undertakes to perform . . . must arise from all his powers united together; everything in isolation is worthless." Goethe calls this "a splended maxim, but difficult to follow." Arnold would certainly have agreed. In *Culture and Anarchy,* he lauded Hellenism, the attempt to achieve "*harmonious* perfection, developing all sides of our humanity" (*CPW,* 5:235). In addition, Goethe observed that "a man, when he speaks, must for the moment be one-sided. There is no communication, no instruction without separation" (*Autobiography,* 12:452; *Werke,* 10:563).[17] Since one can present only one element at a time, *Architectonicè*—creation and organization in terms of the whole rather than single thoughts and images—is paramount (*CPW,* 1:9, 12). The conflict between the need for wholeness and the limitations of expression created a dilemma (see 6r[2], p. 171; cf. 3r[3], p. 154). If man puts aside the desire for expression, Arnold hoped, he can perhaps achieve a sense of the relationship of the part to the whole, or at least see the object as a whole.

In an oft-quoted passage from a letter to Clough, Arnold asserted that modern poets like Keats and Browning "must begin with an Idea of the world in order not to be prevailed over by the world's multitudinousness . . ." (*CL,* 97). The quest for such an Idea was another of Arnold's attempts to overcome the fragmentation of modern society and regain inner wholeness. Ideally, art should be the product of an integrated personality, tapping the full resources of his being and guided by an integrated vision of reality. His advice is really aimed at himself, for as he confesses later in the same letter, in a passage linking it to his fascination with madness: "I have had that desire of fulness [trying to embrace everything and express everything] without respect of the means, which may become almost maniacal . . ." (*CL,* 97). When Arnold's first volume of poems appeared, what disappointed him most was its lack of integration. As he admitted to his sister "K": "my poems are fragments—*i.e.* . . . . I am fragments . . . a person who has any inward completeness can at best only like parts of them . . ." (*UL,* 18; March, 1849°).

In 1877, Arnold reviewed with approval Dr. Ludwig Wiese's analysis of the difference between German and English education: "what distinguishes . . . the German from the English pupil is that the former carries away from his school a sense of the connection of things in what he has studied, the latter a quantity of isolated, unrelated fragments of knowledge . . ." (*CPW*, 8:214). The goal of wholeness looms large in the *YMS* because of Arnold's belief both in its supreme importance and in his own failure to achieve it.

A favorite quotation from Empedocles' *On Nature* attributes man's inability to grasp the whole to the limitations of his senses and his experience (6r[2], 13r[4], pp. 171, 70).[18] Empedocles regarded as mad those who boast that their vision embraces the universe. For Arnold, the only possibility of achieving integration was through being "true / To our own only true, deep-buried selves, / Being one with which we are one with the whole world" ("Empedocles on Etna," II.370–72).[19]

In addition to such general reflections on the condition of man and society, many notes deal with explicitly literary topics. Entries 3 and 4 on 5r and 4v (p. 165) are among his earliest attempts at working out some elements of a poetics. Arnold has already put behind him the idea that the function of the poet is to group objects (*CL*, 99; February, 1849); the idea of poetry as a "magister vitae" (guide to life), with its emphasis upon contents and all-inclusiveness, is not yet in sight (*CL*, 124; October 28, 1852). Here Arnold brings together two different conceptions of literature, without as yet quite unifying them. He begins with what, on the surface, is a rather basic affective theory. Poetry expresses feelings, "the simple feelings of humanity," the kind that Wordsworth had espoused in his preface to *Lyrical Ballads* and that Arnold was to give a classical bias to in his preface to *Poems* (1853), referring to them as "those elementary feelings which subsist permanently in the race, and which are independent of time" (*CPW*, 1:4).[20]

Arnold attributed the "misery" of his times, as we have seen, to man's "incapacity to suffer, enjoy, feel at all, wholly & profoundly" (2r, p. 145).[21] It should now be clear why he also condemned his age for being unpoetical (*CL*, 126).

Arnold next distinguishes between the poet, who by nature seeks to dwell upon his feelings by expressing them harmoniously, and the demands of art, which by implication include the needs of an audience and so require that the feelings be arranged with perfect limpidity for optimum effectiveness.

When Arnold comes to the question of how feelings are to be conveyed, he touches upon the formal requirements of art in only the most general way. The writer arranges his materials (feelings) "so as to produce the fullest most undisturbed effect" (presumably undisturbed by conflicting feelings or thoughts). Despite his emphasis upon feeling, Arnold tried as a poet and later as a critic to oppose subjectivity and to replace it by disinterestedness.

Although there seems to be a bias toward lyric poetry, the entry ends by referring to narrative. Arnold says nothing about the demands of the medium, but he does recognize that feelings cannot be transformed directly into art. His awareness of this difficulty surfaces with the word *circumstances* (5r[3], p. 165), the 1853 preface's "situation" in embryo, or, on a larger scale, an "excellent action" (*CPW*, 1:11). Suddenly Arnold is no longer talking about merely reproducing feelings. The poet, in addition, "deals with" "circumstances." In other words, the poet must imagine an action and empathize with all that it involves. Then he will be able to express the feelings arising from it, having already experienced them in the course of his life. In a letter to Clough of December, 1847, Arnold remarks, in discussing poetic creation: "Shakspeare says that if imagination would apprehend some joy it comprehends some bringer of that joy . . ." (*CL*, 63). Both sketchily anticipate T. S. Eliot's gnomic concept of the "objective correlative."

The call for presenting the facts of experience clearly and truthfully could easily become a call for sincerity, within the framework of a moralistic theory of literature. "Narrative / Is but the pal'd & waning shadow of fact" is an iambic pentameter version of Shelley's comparison of the mind during creation to a fading coal. Both show the influence of Plato's view of *mimesis*. If he does not go so far as Plato in seeing art as only a shadow of a shadow, Arnold here nonetheless regards art as a pale replica of life. But of course, this entry is not an attempt to outline a fully rounded view of art.

In his next entry he notes the harmful influence on poetry of a "cramp'd" life. The implied corollary is that if one leads a rich, noble, well-integrated life, then—if one is an artist—one can produce excellent art. In a Ruskin this can lead to the assertion that only noble men can produce noble art, but for Arnold it was simply the result of his continuing concern for the fullest possible harmonious expansion of all man's powers. It is not surprising, then, that Arnold was soon to inveigh against a poetry that focuses on "the dialogue of the mind with itself" (*CPW*, 1:1). Nothing could be more cramped.

Almost as soon as Arnold began writing in earnest, he became aware that, like any use of language, writing involves the self-contradictory process of imposing fixity and form upon the ever-changing. Moreover, to reflect is to move against the stream, to turn the mind inward and back upon past experience. The writer must accept isolation, for only by ceasing to involve himself in the moment can he reflect; and yet, paradoxically, only by participating and giving himself to the flow of life can he obtain the experience needed to write well. (See 3r[1] and 37r[1][1], pp. 154 and 83, "Resignation" and "Empedocles on Etna.") Arnold understood and also experienced the anguish aroused by the gulf between life and art, experience and language.

In contrasting Tennyson with Shakespeare, the Bible, and the ancient classics, Arnold divides literary discourse into "the naiveté of language & image" and "the large plain manner of thinking & feeling that is in nature" (11r[3], p. 180).[22] The comment anticipates the lectures *On Translating Homer* (1861), where he again links Homer with the Bible, calling the latter the only English book where "perfect plainness of speech is allied with perfect nobleness . . ." (*CPW*, 1:155–56). In associating Tennyson with Keats, the supreme English exemplar of "natural magic," Arnold is paying him only a backhanded compliment, for he regarded natural magic as inferior to those powers of moral and intellectual interpretation possessed by the greatest poets, powers which best serve the needs of modern societies.

In a reflection attributed to Caesar, written about the same time, "the poet" is said to criticize ordinary men of the world "for giving an absolute value to wealth or power" (33r[2], p. 139). Because they consider these proximate goals as ultimate and absolute, they are guilty of worshipping what Arnold was later to call "machinery" (*CPW*, 5:96). The poet, on the other hand, seeks "intellectual or spiritual Vision," an aim that helps him provide intellectual and moral deliverance (*CPW*, 1:19). Both in the *YMS* and in Arnold's poetry, the poet's greatest gift is that of vision, which is unique in its breadth and its detachment.

The poet's goal of "spiritual Vision" is a product of Arnold's humanism. With time, his moral and spiritual concerns deepened, showing that they were no mere reaction to the pressures of the moment. A comment on Shakespeare is especially revealing of his attitude toward the relationship between literature and morality.

> The easy tone of a Shakspeare suits the immoral vulgar: the moralist conscious of his own imperfection & strain, admires it: but what does the poet's own conscience say to it—what would he say at seeing his easy morality erected by Germans & others into a system of life . . . [?] He would say . . . if you mistake my razor edge, you damned pedants, for a bridge, a nice mess you will make of your own & others' walk & conversation. (7r[1], p. 175)

In the terminology of his essay on "Maurice de Guérin," Arnold here examines the nature of a Shakespeare's "moral profundity," his ability to express "with inspired conviction, the ideas and laws of the inward world of man's moral and spiritual nature" (*CPW*, 3:33). By referring to "a Shakspeare," Arnold tries to avoid having Shakespeare's uniqueness vitiate any generalization based upon his practice. To the great mass of his audience—"the immoral vulgar"—his "easy tone" seems easygoing and nondidactic.[23] The moralist, recognizing that Shakespeare's "ease" represents a considerable triumph over difficulties, "admires it." But many academic critics try to derive a moral system from his works. For Shakespeare, morality was largely pragmatic, a difficult balancing act. Therefore, to take his example as a blueprint for others, as a formula to live by, is to fall into serious error. The issue Arnold grapples with here is the nature of the moral utility of the greatest literature. More and more as the years passed, and most clearly in the late essay on "Wordsworth" (*CPW*, 9:46), he insisted that it has an important bearing on how to live. Yet just as he insisted that it was a mistake to look for "a scientific system of thought" in Wordsworth's poetry (*CPW*, 9:48), so here he imagines Shakespeare as objecting to those who seek a moral *system* in his work. Every man has to find his own way. The poet cannot supply answers, but he can animate, compose, elevate, sustain, console, and in those ways have a significant moral influence.

Arnold rarely generalizes about the language of poetry, though he did comment later on the style of a few poets. We have seen him commending language that conveys "the naiveté" of nature (11r[3], p. 180), but that apparently neo-Wordsworthian position begs many of the important questions. Far more significant, though even less explicit, is his attack on the doctrine of correspondence (see pp. 18–19).

Arnold's modern vision of reality, his sense of the gulf between man and the macrocosm, has profound implications for language, especially for the language of poetry. For him, romantic metaphor, image, and symbol were no longer ways of discovering truth. Literal truth must precede metaphor. Analogies, correspondences, metaphors (as the romantics used them)—all lose validity insofar as they cease to reflect the structure of reality. Even when Arnold observes a correspondence, he can only agree to place the two elements side by side. He, of course, realized that this change in outlook made it impossible to go on writing traditional romantic poetry, for he could no more accept a poetics that was false to reality as he experienced it than he could accept the miraculous in Christianity simply because it was consoling. Unfortunately, lacking the ability to transform his medium, he had to work with a language and conventions that were not designed to meet his needs or to express his vision.

Arnold has often been considered simply a late romantic poet who failed to equal the greatest of his predecessors, or more often as one whose heart led him to write romantic poetry while his head drove him to oppose romantic values. His comments here suggest that his break with romanticism was not a superficial product of his understanding or of disagreements about subject matter but a result of his deepest feelings about man's place in the universe. He bore no hostility to the major romantics—and in fact yearned to share their faith and assurance and went on using much of their language and technique—but his radically altered vision of man and the universe prevented him from becoming a romantic poet. Many of his most "romantic" verses—the lyrics of Callicles or the descriptions of the Oxford countryside in "The Scholar-Gipsy" and "Thyrsis"—are only romantic fragments within wholes whose strategies, goals, and outlook are not romantic. To call these poems romantic would be like calling Shakespeare's *Henry IV* (parts 1 and 2) comedies because they contain comic scenes and comic characters.

In the autumn of 1848, Arnold drew up a list of poetic projects for the following year (25r–v, p. 114). One of the reasons why he completed so few of them was probably the reception accorded his first volume of poems published in February, 1849. The initial reaction, according to Arnold, was that readers disliked the meters and the poetic forms. Their reactions made Arnold aware of what was *"practicable."* He admitted that "the objections of people . . . may determine my course as to publishing; e.g. I had thoughts of publishing another volume of short poems next spring . . . [but] at present I shall leave the short poems to take their chance, only writing them when I cannot help it . . ." (Ward, *A Writer's Recollections*, 42–43). He spent much of the early part of the year working on "Lucretius," put aside in the spring for "Empedocles." Then, after returning to Thun in September, came a flood of "unplanned" poems, because he couldn't help writing them.

If one looks at Arnold's considerable accomplishments for 1849, they seem remote from his plans for the year. "Empedocles," which grew until it largely displaced "Lucretius," must have absorbed most of Arnold's poetic energies for the first eight months of the year. Then came the trauma of Switzerland and the overflow of poetry: the beginning of "Tristram and Iseult," the writing of the best of the "Switzerland" poems, and "The Stanzas in Memory of the Author of 'Obermann.' " None of these, his major works for the year, appear on the list. On the other hand, had Arnold brought all his projects to fruition, he would have produced a volume not unlike the poems he actually wrote during the next few years.

Represented on the list are poems with settings remote in time or place, involving Indian temple dancers, an Eastern court, the Breton coast, and Scandinavia of bygone days. Then there are the poems drawing on folklore and legend and others growing out of immediate personal experience, like entry 9, "Thun and vividness of sight and memory compared . . . ." Several poems were to use rather shadowy female characters—Eugenia, Antonia, Meta—who would probably be only foils or bystanders, although occasionally a partial surrogate for their author, as in "To Meta." Then there are the writers from the past—Lucretius, Empedocles, Shelley—used to embody aspects of modern man's psyche and outlook. Arnold lists poems that touch on most of his major themes: the search for an idea of the world, the problem of consciousness and its offbeat offshoot, mesmerism, religious feelings and religious yearnings, man's love for woman, and the limitations and frustrations involved in such love. There are also the conflicts between man's longing for freedom and the limitations imposed by the world and by man's beliefs and attachments, and the choices maturity forces on him. The references to "eternal grief," "pessimism" and hopeless love (entry 12) reflect the elegiac tendency of his verse. The gap between dream and reality, vision and expression, is alluded to (16–17), as is the large question of the choice of career or a way of life—poetic, philosophical, or practical—whether to marry and raise a family (18) or seek fulfilment in the isolation of a cloister (7).

The list, thus, includes much that never came to fruition and omits much that did. Yet it points to the kind of themes, settings, attitudes, and forms that are the hallmark of Arnold's poetry. "Marguerite" simply pushed aside the Eugenias and Antonias. "Tristram and Iseult" preempted other poems on love, career, marriage, children, the life liveable, and limitation. "Obermann" has links with half a dozen of these projects, while "Empedocles on Etna" embraces almost all of Arnold's largest themes. Arnold found new bottles for the old wine, but they resembled the ones he was accustomed to using.

Preparing the ground for "Lucretius" occupies one of the longest entries, which discusses the essential gifts of the dramatic poet (29r–v, p. 135). It begins by stressing the importance of representing others by "observing & recording . . . appearances." Arnold's approach is dualistic. One set of qualities is appropriate for drama; another for other unspecified kinds of poetry. The major oppositions are: drama versus the nondramatic; youth versus maturity; outward appearances versus inward being; vigorous, cheerful versus morbid, dull; absolute versus relative; objective versus subjective, and, by implication, classic versus romantic. The either/or approach unfortunately tends to distort and leads to some contradictions.

With Goethe's distinction between the novel and the drama in mind, Arnold considers Scott a true dramatic poet and Shakespeare a kind of poet-novelist rather than a natural writer for the theater. The importance Goethe attached to the handling of externals in drama comes out clearly in a comment to Eckermann of January 18, 1825, comparing Schiller and himself: "he saw his object only on the outside. . . . [H]e did not take sufficient pains about *motifs* [motives]. . . . I, on the other hand, by too great attention to *motifs,* kept my pieces from the theatre . . . . Schiller's genius was really made for the theatre" (Eckermann, *Conversations,* 85; *Werke,* 24:143).

Arnold begins by speaking of registering appearances, but he assumes that, ideally, the act of representing is by its nature vital, interested, even cheerful: a product of lively curiosity and vigorous senses.[24] His argument logically requires none of these epithets. He is imagining a happy, natural, youthful, untroubled, unfallen dramatic poet, not his usual dramatic idols—Sophocles, Molière, and (though a bad model) Shakespeare—but Scott! In other words, here is Callicles, not the lyric warbler but the lively, unreflective dramatist (the kind of poet that T. S. Eliot similarly dreamed of as existing before "the dissociation of sensibility"). Empedocles is, of course, his opposite, or rather his mature and fallen counterpart, the poet distracted by his "own thoughts on man and society." Callicles' lyrics present myths in lively and sensuous form. Empedocles, on hearing them, "put[s] himself in the place of the person represented." This entry seems to point to "Empedocles on Etna" as a portrait of two kinds of poets: not so much the traditional romantic singer (Callicles) and the introspective modern philosopher (Empedocles), but the classical, objective dramatic poet and the romantic, subjective poet—the former, healthy; the latter, sick.

Although Arnold's comments have their origin in his reading of Goethe, their emphases differ widely, as Goethe's assessment of the Bard in "Shakespeare ad Finitum" makes plain: "No one despised the outer costume of men more than he; but he understood well the inner man. . . . [I]t is just his neglect of the outer form that makes his works so vital" (Spingarn, 177; *Werke*, 14:758–59). Arnold, however, agreed with Goethe's conclusion that "Shakespeare belongs by necessity in the annals of poetry; in the annals of the theatre he appears only by accident" (Spingarn, 185; *Werke*, 14:765). By focusing on "dramatic effect," Arnold minimizes "the representation of . . . the inner man," which was for Goethe the central feature of poetry (*Dichtung und Wahrheit*, 7:227; *Werke*, 10:291). In questioning the importance of the poet's insight into the inner life of man, Arnold is denigrating one of his own greatest gifts and revealing why he was better able to produce a dramatic poem like "Empedocles on Etna" than a play like the long-meditated "Lucretius."[25]

Parts of the entry obviously point toward the preface to *Poems* (1853). The opposition between the "cheerful & unbiassed observing & recording of appearances" and "our occupation with our own thoughts" provides the parameters for Arnold's later assertion that in the age of Empedocles "the calm, the cheerfulness, the disinterested objectivity have disappeared; the dialogue of the mind with itself has commenced . . ." (*CPW*, 1:1). Both statements emphasize the value of representation: "Any accurate representation" is interesting partly because it adds to our "knowledge" (*CPW*, 1:2). This brings to the surface one of Arnold's major objections to the emphasis on the "inward being of man." Being "unseen," it "can never be absolutely rendered" ("represented"). Some of Arnold's best poetry employs the romanticist's strategy of projecting the self into others, but Arnold's comments here suggest that he was suspicious of this artistic procedure as a mode of achieving knowledge, for he craved what was objective and absolute, and such poetry provided neither (cf. 36v[2], p. 112).

The 1853 preface adds the important proviso that the representation, in addition to being accurate, must also contribute to man's happiness; it must "inspirit and rejoice" (*CPW*, 1:2). In 1848–49,

Arnold implied that this goal would be achieved as a result of the cheerful, vigorous, and lively spirit in which the representation took place. By 1853, he came to believe that the object represented—"an excellent action"—was the essential source of joy (*CPW*, 1:4).

The search for an excellent action led Arnold to a startling reversal. Because he believed that most of the best subjects are ancient, one would expect a Victorian writer to be at a disadvantage, but not so, says Arnold:

> The externals of a past action, indeed, he cannot know with the precision of a contemporary; but his business is with its essentials. The outward man . . . he cannot accurately figure to himself; but neither do they essentially concern him. His business is with their inward man; with their feelings and behaviour in certain tragic situations, which engage their passions as men; these have in them nothing local and casual; they are as accessible to the modern poet as to a contemporary. (*CPW*, 1:5)

In reversing his earlier insistence upon the importance of appearances rather than depth, he is thinking both of epic narrative and of drama. There is no question, however, about his target in "On the Modern Element in Literature" (1857), where he points to the episode of Dido in the *Aeneid* as coming closest to drama because "locality and manners are nothing . . . [;] persons and characters are everything" (*CPW*, 1:35).[26]

More narrowly, there is an entry analyzing the character of Empedocles ($27r^1$–v^1, p. 137). In choosing him, Arnold believed he was following the lead of dramatists like Aeschylus and Sophocles, who dealt with figures from the remote past: "into these figures of the old world is poured all the fulness of life and of thought which the new world had accumulated" (*CPW*, 1:31).

This entry ignores Simon Karsten's portrait of Empedocles as a proud polymath and instead focuses on the dilemma of a solitary for whom the life of the mind is uppermost. Without either the limitations or the consolations that can come with religious belief, Empedocles possesses many of the characteristics that Arnold later attributed to the disinterested critic whose mind plays freely upon all subjects and who "see[s] the object as in itself it really is" (*CPW*, 3:268, 261). That he is something of a seer, the emphasis on vision, sight, and spectacle makes clear, but he lacks the steadiness and assured vision of the ideal poet, the Sophocles of "To a Friend." In fact, his vision of the stark, unadorned truth proves to be "mind-tasking" and eventually "overtask[ing]." Arnold notes more clearly in the *YMS* than in his poem that "joy, grandeur, spirit, and animated life" have not yet been completely extinguished in Empedocles and that he hopes to preserve them by dying. Part of this, of course, is simply a consequence of traditional Stoic ethics, which regards death as preferable to the loss of integrity. The two stanzas intended for Empedocles' homily, added to the *YMS* a year or two later (26r, p. 209), are also more Stoic (and existential) than genuinely Empedoclean and reflect Arnold's own outlook.

Because modern life seemed to him to consist of a multiplicity of fragments, he sought intellectual deliverance by attempting to discover the order he believed must underlie them. The *YMS* thus provides a record of the early stages of Arnold's search for meaning. In these fragments we hear a voice that is modern, not in Arnold's sense, but in ours. More than seven decades before Yeats's vision of the disintegration of civilization, the *YMS* attests to Arnold's awareness that things have already fallen apart and that the center is not holding. Arnold characteristically refused to pretend that it was otherwise, but he also never abandoned his quest for wholeness, spared the knowledge that artists yet unborn would continue to see man as a fragmented being facing a fragmented universe. The *YMS* itself is, justifiably, also a heap of fragments, not shored against ruins, but awaiting a unifying act of imagination.

NOTES

1. All are available in the Allotts' splendidly annotated edition of the poems (*P*). The transcription and dating of these manuscripts, however, are not always reliable, and Arnold's punctuation, capitalization, and spelling

have been revised to conform to the editorial guidelines of the Longman series.

2. Some of Goethe's ideas originally reached A. through the mediation of Carlyle, but by his Lansdowne years A. was deep in Goethe's collected works.

3. Sheet 16 (p. 95) contains quotations from *Dido, Queen of Carthage* by Marlowe (and Nashe?). In all of them, supernatural powers or events determine the destiny of mortals.

4. Later he quoted Spinoza with approval: *"Our desire is not that nature may obey us, but, on the contrary, that we may obey nature"* (*Tractatus Theologico-Politicus* [*CPW*, 3:176]; cf. 21r²[2] and 5v[2], pp. 102 and 168.) A genius, however, may find ways of making the laws of nature serve his own ends (32r[1], p. 89).

5. See also Burke, *Correspondence*, 3:304, which A. had been reading June 1847/48 (*N-Bs*, 442). Cf. the concluding paragraph of A.'s preface to *Poems* (1853); *CPW*, 1:15.

6. A.'s earliest published poem, "Alaric at Rome," was the first of many to make use of Rome.

7. Cf. "the confused alarms" of "ignorant armies" in "Dover Beach," lines 36–37.

8. Cf. letter to Clough of September 23, 1849, which refers to his struggle against external distractions and his revulsion not only against these "damned times" but also against his own self (*CL*, 111).

9. This attitude seems to have much in common with Martin Heidegger's existential vision of man's *Geworfenheit* ("thrownness") in *Sein und Zeit* (1927).

10. In *Lazare*, Barbier also depicts industrial slavery, the grim alternative to madness in the modern world of "A Summer Night." A.'s poetry rarely deals with this topic, and even in this poem his most moving image is of the madman, the escaped prisoner, who, amid the severest of tempests, seeks to make "for some false, impossible shore," line 69.

11. A. deplores the obsessive behavior of the monomaniac but also complains that man rarely is able to develop all sides of himself. Society, by bombarding each of us with a multiplicity of stimuli, makes it impossible to pursue a single goal and be true to our central self.

12. Entry 1a on sheet 2r (p. 145), which appears on the same sheet with one of the two passages from "Tristram and Iseult," part III, included in the *YMS* (2v and 10v, pp. 149–50 and 157), also throws light on these lines.

13. The concept of affinity is also relevant to the island image in "To Marguerite—Continued." The poem explores not simply human isolation but the limitations imposed by one's affinities. If one could touch on more, expand one's borders, then memory and knowledge would expand as well.

14. Goethe's novel also deals briefly with the problem of learning and memory. Ottilie is unable to learn things by rote like other girls, but once she

can relate something to "former experience" and "can find the connecting links," then "nothing is too difficult for her comprehension" (*Elective Affinities,* 30; *Werke,* 9:33). This is another sort of affinity, the kind that used to be called "relevance."

15. A.'s concerns here are with us still, but we express them in different terms. The concluding sentence of Carol Christ's *The Finer Optic,* without referring to A., brings out what underlies his comments here: "The leap from a system of assumed correspondences to the observation of a world of particulars admits the possibility that the universe is not divine but arbitrary, and the only proof of revelations that remains is the intensity of personal experience." In short, A. is dealing with the consequences of what J. Hillis Miller calls "The Disappearance of God." Frank Kermode provides an even broader perspective, from which A.'s reflections become "a way of recognizing the gulf between being and knowing." Correspondences and juxtapositions, which give so much pleasure and assurance, are what Kermode calls "concord-fictions": "Stoic physics, biblical typology, Copenhagen quantum theory, are all different, but all use concord-fictions and assert complementarities. Such fictions meet a need" (*The Sense of an Ending,* 62).

16. Likewise, genuine free will depends upon the almost impossible task of knowing oneself ("Once read thy own breast right, / And thou hast done with fears" ("Empedocles on Etna," I.ii.142–43) and the only slightly less elusive goal of being oneself: "he / Who finds himself, loses his misery!" ("Self-Dependence," lines 31–32). See note on these lines in *P* (150).

17. A. read and took notes on Goethe's autobiography between late 1847 and mid-1848 (dating based upon handwriting), returning to it in the late winter or spring of 1849 (letter to his mother, May 7, 1849°[*L*]).

18. Cf. *Gespräche mit Goethe,* October 15, 1825: Man's "faculties are not sufficient to measure the actions of the universe" (Eckermann, *Conversations,* 120; *Werke,* 24:164).

19. A. would have found a similar outlook in the Bhagavad Gita and in Goethe, who remarked to Riemer (Mar. 19, 1807): "in all things the individual exists for the whole and vice versa, because the individual is at the same time the whole. Nature, however diverse her manifestations, is always one—a unity . . ." (Weigand, 90; *Werke,* 22:441).

20. In April, 1850, A. eulogized Wordsworth in "Memorial Verses" for the power of his poetry to "make us feel," line 67. Nearly three decades later, A. stood by that claim and expanded it (*CPW,* 9:51). This attitude toward poetry has much in common with that of the wise bards in "The Strayed Reveller," who "become what [they] sing," line 234.

21. Cf. "The Scholar-Gipsy," line 173 and *P,* 365n. The lack of wholeness and profundity in man's feelings are the affective counterpart of the fragmentation of knowledge.

22. Only the greatest writers are able to combine language with thought and feeling to achieve wholeness. A. divides language and imagery from

thought and feeling, ostensibly only for the sake of analysis, anticipating his concept of "The Grand Style," first mentioned somewhat ironically in referring to "Memorial Verses" (*CL,* 115).

23. Much of literature's moral effect is achieved through style: "For the style is the expression of the nobility of the poet's character, as his matter is the expression of the richness of his mind: but on men character produces as great an effect as mind" (*CL,* 101).

24. Earlier, in a different context, it suited him in writing to Clough to despise the value of registering appearances: "to *solve* the Universe as you try to do is as irritating as Tennyson's dawdling with its painted shell is fatiguing to me to witness . . ." (*CL,* 63).

25. The 1853 preface is often taken as marking the beginning of the end for A. the poet, who there turns against the sources of his poetic strength. But that is only the first time he did so in public. Here, and in the letters to Clough, he repeatedly expresses dissatisfaction with the principles that underlie his best poetry.

26. For A.'s interest in Dido, see 16r (p. 95).

The Text and Physical Features of the Manuscripts and of the Bound Volume

Except for obvious slips of the pen, this edition reproduces Arnold's punctuation, spelling, and capitalization. Even the ° symbol (instead of *sic* or indicating a corrected date) has been used sparingly in the hope that readers will assume that the text has been transcribed with care. Generally Arnold's revisions of his prose have not been noted.

Spelling and abbreviations: Arnold often does not bother to write carefully such endings as *-ing,* and *-ion.* Where his intentions are obvious, the full spelling has been supplied. In his poetry, however when the final *-ed* does not constitute a separate syllable and is represented in his published work as *'d,* Arnold sometimes writes simply *d,* as in *turnd.* The edition lets stand his remarkably rare careless misspellings.

Arnold consistently uses the spelling *Shakspeare.*

He regularly uses conventional abbreviations: & for *and*; wch for *which*; and tho: for *though.*

Foreign words and phrases: Arnold normally does not differentiate foreign words and phrases from native ones, either by underlining them or by enclosing them in quotation marks. Nor does he always bother to include accents. These omissions are generally a sign of familiarity rather than of ignorance.

Capitalization: It is not always possible to be certain of Arnold's intentions, because some of his capital letters are only larger versions of his lowercase letters. Position and syntax are not infallible guides, for he does not always capitalize the beginning of entries or of sentences, and he sometimes capitalizes important nouns, probably following his father's eighteenth-century practice and that of the Germans.

39

Punctuation: The entries are sparsely punctuated, but a major departure from modern practice is Arnold's use of the colon, especially at the end of a clause where we would use a semicolon or a period. He also uses colons to indicate abbreviations: for example, "Ball: Coll:" for Balliol College.[1] In drafts of some poems, he uses a dash to separate clauses and to indicate a pause.

Transcription of Arnold's punctuation cannot be totally free from error. It is sometimes impossible to be sure that a punctuation mark is supposed to be a period, a comma, or a dash. Spots in the paper can also be mistaken for punctuation marks, especially when they occur where one would expect to find a punctuation mark.

Paper: No two sheets are the same size, except in the notebook (sheets 1–14). As Lord Lansdowne's private secretary, Arnold was free to help himself to whatever odds and ends were available, just as he frequently used Education Department stationery for letters and articles after he became a school inspector.

Watermarks: Watermarks occur on eleven sheets. Five identify their manufacturer: C. Ansell (31), Fellows (23), Ruse & Turner (24), and J. Whatman (16, 20). Three others (15, 19, 33) have fragmentary designs.

The few watermarked dates have not been very helpful in dating the manuscripts. Three sheets (20, 21, and 31) have only the first two digits. Another sheet (32) has no final digit, 184—. Two sheets are dated 1837 (23 and 33), suggesting that Arnold sometimes used old supplies. One sheet (24) is dated 1846 and another (16), 1847. Sheet 31, which handwriting dates March, 1848/49, bears the name C. ANSELL, used on paper in 1837 and again from 1846 to 1854.

The Bound Volume: The *YMS* is bound in full dark blue crushed levant morocco with three gilt lines around the edges of the front cover as well as a decorative narrow gilt border inside the covers.

The cover has inscribed on its spine: UN- / PUBLISH / -ED / POEMS / ETC. MATTHEW / ARNOLD The front cover bears the following inscription in gilt lettering:

ORIGINAL MANUSCRIPTS

OF

UNPUBLISHED POEMS,

NOTES

ON LECTURES ETC.

BY

MATTHEW ARNOLD

The volume is contained in a light blue, lined box with the same inscription on its edge as on the spine of the volume.

The *YMS* consists of thirty-seven sheets set into pages numbered from 1 to 73 (with numerous omissions). The sheets used to frame the manuscripts bear the watermark "ORIGINAL / TURKEY MILL / KENT" of James Whatman.

Lines 1 and 6 of the title page are in red, underlined in black (see p. 42). All the other lines are in black underlined in red.

C. B. Tinker and H. F. Lowry, in their *Commentary*, report all that is known of the provenance of the *YMS*: Tinker purchased the volume from Dr. Gabriel Wells of New York. Lowry first mentioned it in print in his edition of Arnold's letters to Clough (1932). The following year Tinker discussed sheet 25 in the *Yale Review*. It is likely, then, that he purchased the volume no later than 1931. Probably Wells or some other book dealer assembled the volume, had it bound, and composed the text of the title page. Such phrases as "*a Note Book / Used by the Poet*" and "*IN THE HANDWRITING / OF*" suggest that the title was invented by a bookseller rather than by a member of the Arnold family. Wells and the family patronized the same binder.

Gabriel Wells (1861–1946), a Hungarian by birth, came to the United States about 1897. For a time he specialized in fine bindings. Several of his ventures brought him much attention but not until after World War I: he purchased an incomplete Gutenberg Bible in 1921 and disposed of sections individually; and he sold several Shakespeare first folios, as well as the manuscripts of the Browning

Unpublished Poems

—

Notes on Lectures
and other matter
In the Handwriting
of
Matthew Arnold

—

Contained in a Note Book
Used by the Poet at
Balliol College, Oxford

1843

The title page of the Yale Manuscript.

love letters and of Hardy's *Far from the Madding Crowd.* Later he had a controlling financial interest in the London bookshop of Henry Sotheran and Co., then bookseller to His Majesty, as well as bookbinder and publisher.

The firm of Rivière and Son bound the *YMS.* It was perhaps the most distinguished English bookbinder of the nineteenth century. The firm worked on the Chatsworth library, bound Shakespeare folios and the large illustrated catalogs for the Great Exhibition of 1851, restored and bound the Domesday Book in 1870, and was patronized by monarchs from Victoria through George V. The craftsman who, around the turn of the century, regularly did the most important engrossing for the firm undoubtedly penned the title page of the *YMS.*[2] Rivière seems not to have used paper with the Turkey Mill watermark after about 1920.

Pagination and Dating

Most of the framing sheets are numbered in pencil. The manuscripts themselves contain tiny sheet numbers in the lower left corner of the recto of each sheet, probably added by a librarian. This edition focuses on the sheet numbers, because the page numbers are incomplete and illogical; but page numbers are recorded when they exist, and, when they do not exist, are supplied in brackets (pp. 55–56).[3] When a sheet or page number is omitted—for example, 15v—it is blank. Superscript numerals refer to double sheets.

This edition is arranged chronologically. All entries on the same page are discussed together under the date of the earliest major entry (not always the entry at the top of the manuscript page). Whenever a page includes an entry written more than a year before or after the one that determines the page's chronological place in this edition, the entry is cross-listed chronologically under its own date.

Those who wish to ignore the chronological arrangement can readily reconstruct the volume as it stands from the listing on pages 55–56.

The order of the pages is less significant than their dates. Unlike the page order in the bound volume, the chronological arrangement of this edition should not mislead anyone who keeps in mind that most of the dates span a year. An apparent difference of three months between two entries is not significant, because entries dated June, 1849/50, and September, 1849/50, for example, overlap for ten months. No inferences about chronology should be drawn from the fact that one page precedes another in this edition. A page dated, for example, July, 1849/50, could have been written after one dated June, 1850/51.

Calligraphy has long been used to assign anonymous manuscripts to their historical period and to determine whether manuscripts of known authorship were written during the writer's youth, maturity, or old age. A relatively recent development, however, is the use of calligraphy to date manuscripts within a year or even less.[4]

The basic unit of analysis is a letter of the alphabet. This, in turn, is subdivided depending upon its position at the beginning, middle, or end of a word.

Precision in dating is of course partly a function of the amount of dated material available. Without at least three thousand words a year in dated manuscripts accurate results are difficult to obtain.

A number of variables complicate the task of comparing samples of calligraphy. Manuscripts written with a pencil differ from those written with a pen. A change in pen or pen point also affects the calligraphy. Health, mood, and fatigue likewise influence handwriting, as does the nature of the manuscript and the purpose for which it was written. The calligraphy of a formal letter or a fair copy of a poem will normally differ from that used in dashing off a note to a friend or writing a first draft of a poem. These variables, however, merely make the task of analyzing calligraphy difficult, not impossible. Although comparisons among homogeneous manuscripts naturally produce the most reliable results, valid comparisons are possible among heterogeneous materials. For example, a single informal manuscript containing a long quotation, normally copied with care, enables an analyst to observe the differences between a kind of rough draft and a contemporary fair copy. For Matthew Arnold, fair copies are regressive in their calligraphy, while his rough drafts are innovative and reveal the direction in which his handwriting is developing.

The apparent chronological differences between a fair copy and a rough draft by Arnold is about a year. Fortunately, a few telltale signs always reveal that his fair copies are of later date than most of their features would otherwise lead one to suppose.

Each manuscript has been analyzed on a separate sheet of ruled paper on which lines are provided for the letters of the alphabet and for any commonly used symbols, such as the ampersand (&). Theoretically every occurrence of every letter should be traced on this sheet, using a lighted box with a glass top. Because transcribing even a single manuscript in this way is extremely time consuming, one makes shortcuts. To make them intelligently, prior study of the calligraphy is essential. Some letters vary little from year to year. Other letters appear too infrequently to be useful, for example, capital Q, K, X, V, and Z. Medial letters, except for distinctive combinations such as *th*, can normally be eliminated, thus saving considerable time. They generally show less variation from year to year than initial or final letters, and of course they are affected by both the letter that precedes and the one that follows them. An examination of medial d, f, h, p and y in hundreds of pages of Arnold manuscripts yielded little that was helpful for dating. After deciding which letters and symbols to analyze, one can duplicate lined forms with only the relevant letters indicated in the left-hand margin and some blank lines for later additions.

Often it is not only easier but also more useful to subdivide individual letters into major categories. Once these have been chosen, it is enough to trace one example of each category and then simply note how often each occurs. Four or five categories for any one letter are normally enough. Finer distinctions are unnecessary, if one has chosen categories that cover the range of variables. Obviously judgment based upon experience is necessary in deciding how many different variables to use and which letters to analyze.

Although a letter may vary from document to document and from year to year, it sometimes varies in a random way and is therefore useless as a clue to dating and can be dropped from further analysis. Arnold's final y's are extremely variable, but the variations depend more upon his mood and his purpose than upon the date. In Arnold, initial letters are the most revealing, while capital letters are much more useful than their relative rarity would lead one to suppose.

Within a period of months Arnold sometimes drastically altered the way he formed a letter and then might make no change in it for years. Yet although few letters retain their importance for dating throughout his career, in any given year some letters will differ significantly from those of the year before. These, then, become the major indicators for determining whether a manuscript was written during that year. Although it sometimes happens that a variant will disappear only to reappear some years later, the overall configuration of the other letters will indicate whether this is the first or second appearance of the variant.

Once a representative group of documents has been analyzed and transcribed, the sheets need to be studied carefully letter by letter to discover which letters are the most useful for dating. After this, one can proceed still more selectively in transcribing letters from the remaining manuscripts.

In this kind of analysis of calligraphy *similarities are much more important than differences.* Differences are the norm, similarities the exception. Therefore if every major variant of a single letter in an undated manuscript has its counterpart in the dated manuscripts of a given year, one has a clue to the dating. If all the letters of the manuscript fall into categories occurring within that year, the date of the document is established. Despite the fact that each individual letter is unique in some small way, if a manuscript is to be convincingly assigned to a particular year, the *pattern* of *all* its letters must be appropriate to the categories for that year, and unusual variants must be of a kind that are at least possible for that date. For instance, if the staff of a letter in successive years formed an angle with the horizontal of 30°, 60°, and 90°, a staff at an angle of 40° could easily be dated by its place in the sequence, even though no other examples of a staff at this angle existed in dated documents. Because patterns for all the letters, surprisingly, do fit in this way, it is usually possible to date manuscripts with a high degree of confidence.

To demonstrate the use of calligraphy to date entries in "The Yale Manuscript," ideally one ought to illustrate with a great many sheets

filled with individual letters of the alphabet traced from dated samples
of Arnold's handwriting. Table 1 is a modest substitute for many
pages of examples. It lists the letters and symbols that have proven to
be the most useful in dating a representative manuscript from this
collection, "And that golden fruited strand" ["The Pillars of the Universe,"] (sheet 18r).

Analysis began with all twelve capital letters and twenty-one lowercase letters, symbols, and combinations. Most proved to be of little
or no use for dating because they can be found throughout the period, and so they are not included in table 1. Virtually all the available
dated manuscripts of poems, letters, and diaries for the years
1847–52 have been drawn upon for comparison.[5] Manuscripts for
other years were eliminated because they had too little in common
with the handwriting of "The Pillars of the Universe."

Where the similarity between a dated letter and one in the poem
is sufficiently close, a + has been entered on the chart along with the
month in which the document containing the match was written. Personal judgment, of course, ultimately determines whether the similarity is "sufficiently close."

		Pillars of the Universe	1847	1848	1849	1850	1851	1852
1	f	Norm			Mar Norm	May Norm		
2	G				+ Mar	+ Oct (Fair Copy)	+ Jan June	
3	g			+ July	+ Feb	+ May	+ Jan Apr	+ Jan Apr
4	Th			+ Fall	+ Feb	+ Jan		
5	&				Mar + July		+ Jan	
TOTALS			0	2	5	4	3	1

Table 1

47

And that golden fingered strand
Near where Atlas hath his stand
Bearing on his shoulder broad
Earth, & Heaven's star-ofayled load,
In the farthest western wild.
Far eastward, where uppil'd
To maintain the Caspian free
From the Euxine sea
In his light austere
Great Elbruz whitens clear:
Bearing in his enlovie'd Stone
The too-daring island bones

18

"The Pillars of the Universe."

Table 1 also includes examples of letters from the poem labeled "norm." A "norm" is a category or calligraphic subtype that includes more than half the occurrences of an individual letter of the alphabet. When this category is also dominant in at least one document in a given year, the table includes a + and the month the document was written. The category may occur throughout the period covered by this table, but only in the years marked with a + is it ever the norm, as it is in the poem. Where categories are involved, precise matching is not required.

Matching demands enough familiarity with Arnold's handwriting to recognize unusual configurations. Where there is no match in a given year, the table includes the variant that comes closest to matching. The key features used to determine the matches in table 1 are as follows:

1. Initial *f* (norm) [lines 5, 6, 7, 8]: a loop at the top and another to the left at the bottom (often very narrow).
2. *G* [line 10]: an elongated loop at the top, a sharply pointed middle, and a small loop to the left at the bottom.
3. Initial *g* [line 1]: straight or slightly convex downstroke and a straight upstroke to the right at roughly a 30° angle, with almost no overlapping.
4. *Th* [lines 6, 12]: joined at top of the *h* with no overlap. The beginning of the *T* is looped but not quite closed.
5. *&* [line 4]: The downstroke is at an angle of less than 20° from the vertical, and the angle between the downstroke and the endstroke is about 90°. The endstroke does not curve after crossing the downstroke.

Two letters that have only a limited value for dating the poem have not been included in table 1: *A* and a subclass of *e*. Together they tend to rule out 1847 and the first four months of 1848:

a. *A* (norm): The norm before May, 1848, resembles the printed letter *A* in coming to a point at the top. From that time on, most are rounded at the top and somewhat elliptical, as in lines 1 and 2.

b. *e:* There are two major subclasses or categories of *e*, the common looped *e* and the epsilon. Examples of both occur in line 6. In the poem, 10 percent of the *e*'s are epsilons [lines 5, 6, 8(2)]. In 1847, epsilons make up a maximum of 7 percent of the *e*'s. Thereafter the range increases from a steady minimum of 2–3 percent up to maxima of 12½ percent (1848), 18½ percent (1849), 20 percent (1850), 25 percent (1851). This seems to suggest that the poem was written closer to 1848 than to 1851, although a 10 percent frequency can be found at any time after 1847.

Table 1 also does not include the *th* combination, which is probably the most important single calligraphic indicator for dating this poem. Arnold usually lifts his pen or pencil to cross his *t*'s, but in the forties and early fifties he sometimes formed the *th* combination without making a separate stroke as in the poem, lines 1, 2, 4, 5. The percentage of all *th*'s that this category constitutes is tabulated below:

November, 1847–March 15, 1848 16 percent average
March 20–December 31, 1848 38 percent average (range: 10–74 percent)
January–September, 1849 30 percent average (range: 9–75 percent)
October, 1849–December 31, 1850 usually less than 20 percent (fair copies: 29 percent and 50 percent)
1851 0 norm (February–March maximum: 14 percent)
1852 0

Because this special *th* configuration occurs 57 percent of the time in "The Pillars of the Universe," this indicator alone would seem to suggest a date between March 20, 1848, and the end of September, 1849, the only period when the category at times became the norm. Table 1 points to the February–March, 1849, period as the most likely date for the poem. (The evidence may be somewhat skewed because many dated manuscripts are available for these dates.) This date does not conflict with the results given by the two letters and the combination discussed above. *All* the calligraphic configurations in the poem can be found during this period or could reasonably be expected then. To give some leeway, one normally provides a range of five or six months before and after the presumed date. Consequently, the limits September, 1848–September, 1849 have been chosen.[6]

Although certainly not infallible, the dating of entries by means of calligraphic analysis enables us to make more precise than formerly their connections with Arnold's other writings and so makes it possible to trace his development with greater accuracy.[7]

The Notebook, Sheets 1–14

Along with a discarded thin board or paper cover, the first fourteen sheets of the *YMS* once constituted the "Note Book" referred to on the title page. The reasons for this assertion are presented in this section.

All the sheets are exactly the same length, 20.0 cm (7⅞ in.). (Their widths differ slightly, probably a result of the way the sheets were separated.) They resemble those in Arnold's notebook of June, 1847, where the sheets are about 7 mm wider and longer.

All fourteen sheets consist of oyster white, wove, unwatermarked paper. They are the only unfolded sheets (with the single exception of sheet 34, written several years after all the others).

Sheets 1 and 14, the first and last in the notebook, are the only ones of this group that are blank on one side. Both have brown sticker marks at the top and bottom of one side of the page and a fold mark running almost the entire length of the sheet. Both also have faint dark "borders" about 1.5 mm wide on three sides, probably the remains of paste. These sheets are also slightly grayer than the other twelve. These features suggest that these two sheets were endpapers, and so, technically, should not be considered pages at all. Page 1r (really 1v) originally would have faced 2r.

The inscription in ink on the first sheet takes the same form and occupies the same position on the page as that in a notebook of Arnold's owned by Mr. Arnold Whitridge. The inscription reads: "M. Arnold. / Ball: Coll: / 1844." (Arnold inscribed it when he bought the notebook, but he did not begin using it until three years later. The outside cover bears the date June, 1847, and the handwriting also indicates that Arnold made his first substantive entries in 1847.)

Verbal links tie together sheets 3–5, 6–10, and 11–12. There are no connections of this kind between any of the twenty-three sheets that were not part of the notebook.

Except for two entries made later and three revisions of single words, also made later, Arnold used a pencil throughout the notebook. All but three of the other sheets are in ink.

Five or six of the sheets of the notebook contain entries made more than a year apart. There are no such gaps between entries on the remaining sheets (except, again, for the last sheet, which contains two early fragments in pencil). Arnold was more likely to return to make entries on a partially filled page of a notebook than on a loose sheet of paper.

Filling in the notebook: After writing on the endpapers and on one adjacent page in the years 1843–45/46, Arnold added less than a page until well into 1849, when he began to make frequent entries through 1850.

He first filled in the front endpaper and then turned to the back double spread, filling in 13v and 14r (the endpaper). Next he worked toward the front, writing on 13r, 12v, 11v, and 12r. Then he moved to the front again and worked toward the back. Thereafter no clear pattern emerges, except that he felt free to move backward or forward. One indication of his habit of sometimes writing from the back toward the front occurs at the bottom of 5r: he begins a sentence there and completes it at the bottom of the preceding sheet, 4v. (The pages cannot be reversed because 4r is a continuation of 3v.) At the end, Arnold added occasional short entries wherever he could find space and, if possible, an appropriate context, as on 1r, 3r, and 13r. Unlike the miscellaneous sheets, in the notebook Arnold left blank almost no spaces large enough for an average entry.

The Miscellaneous Sheets, 15–37

Because of the apparently miscellaneous character of the *YMS* and the fact that, long after Arnold's death, its contents were arranged in a way that he could not have anticipated and probably would not have sanctioned, one might assume that someone took the notebook and added enough miscellaneous papers to make a volume. Judging from its contents, however, this is unlikely. These papers belong together, and Arnold seems to have kept them together.

The notebook has a kind of unity, even though it includes a variety of materials. Arnold must have believed that they had enough in common to justify being put into this notebook rather than into one of the others he was keeping at the same time. He used this notebook from about 1843–46 and again, much more intensively, from about the middle of 1849 until the end of 1852 (although there is little for the last two years). Arnold wrote eighteen of the miscellaneous sheets during the hiatus between 1847 and mid-1849, although there was some overlapping in 1849, when he began to return to this notebook as his major literary workbook. Of the remaining five sheets, three were written after the notebook was too full for them. This leaves only two sheets to account for: 23 and 35. The former contains one brief entry about God and was probably jotted down at a moment when the notebook was not handy. Perhaps the same explanation can be offered for the other sheet, although it obviously took longer to write. Its topics are clearly consonant with the rest.

Simply put, the loose sheets were almost all written either at a time when Arnold was not using his notebook regularly (1847–mid-1849) or after he had filled it.

Finally, with the exception of the late sheet of materials for "Lucretius," all the loose sheets have been folded, usually more than once, so that they could fit into a small envelope. It is likely that Arnold himself put them into one or more envelopes and then, perhaps, either tucked them inside the notebook or put everything into a large container. Whoever had these manuscripts bound probably found the materials already collected, but not arranged in sequence.

NOTES

1. Instead of hyphenating at the end of a line, A. often uses a colon and another to begin the next line. This usage has not been retained because this edition does not reproduce the line divisions of A.'s prose.
2. The company bound 90 percent of the books in Thomas J. Wise's Ashley Library. An examination of thirty-five of its volumes bound by Rivière and containing special title pages reveals calligraphy very similar to that on the title page of the *YMS*.
3. All the rectos have page numbers, but from 48 on the versos do not, except for 72. From page 19 on, the odd-numbered pages are *followed* by the next lower even number (except that 72 follows 71). Thus, for example, page 20 follows page 21. The first three pages of a double sheet usually have only one page number.
4. See Theodora Ward's analysis of the handwriting of Emily Dickinson in Thomas H. Johnson's edition of *The Poems* (1955), 1:xlix–lix, and the Pilgrim Edition of *The Letters of Charles Dickens,* (1965–) especially 1:xxiv–xxv, in which more than two-thirds of the letters were originally undated.
5. The number of pages of manuscript used is as follows: 1847, 58; 1848, 86; 1849, 30; 1850, 28; 1851, 159; 1852, 92.
6. Although the table might seem to suggest a slightly later rather than a slightly earlier date, to include all of 1849 and none of 1848, for example, would challenge the evidence of the *th* formation, which is especially important because it is well represented in all the dated documents in a way that most of the other indicators are not.
7. For brief additional comments on the method and its application to "Dover Beach," see Ullmann, "Dating Through Calligraphy," *SB* 26 (1973): 19–36.

The Yale Manuscript
Text and Commentary

YMS Sheet	YMS Page	This Edition	YMS Sheet	YMS Page	This Edition
1r	1	57	16v	30	95
2r	3	145	17r	33	142
2v	4	149–50	17v	32	142
3r	5	154	18r	35	126
3v	6	194–95	19r^1	37[r^1]	104
4r	7	195	19v^1	37[v^1]	106
4v	8	163, 165	20r	39	207
5r	9	165	20v	38	207
5v	10	168	21r^1	41[r^1]	102
6r	11	171	21v^1	41[v^1]	102
6v	12	178	21r^2	41[r^2]	102
7r	13	175, 178	22r	43	79
7v	14	199	22v	42	81
8r	15	199, 203	23r	45	192
8v	16	182–83	24r^1	47[r^1]	75
9r	17	183, 186	24v^1	47[v^1]	75
9v	[17v]	186, 189	24r^2	47[r^2]	75–76
10r	19	189	25r	49	114
10v	18	157	25v	[48]	114
11r	21	180	26r	51	209
11v	20	131–32	27r^1	53[r^1]	137
12r	23	132	27v^1	53[v^1]	137
12v	22	128	28r	55	122
13r	25	70	28v	[54]	123
13v	24	64	29r	57	135
14r	27	68	29v	[56]	135
15r	29	100	30r	59	92
16r	31	95	30v	[58]	93

YMS Sheet	YMS Page	This Edition		YMS Sheet	YMS Page	This Edition
31r	61	109		36r	71	98
31v	[60]	109		36v	72	112
32r	63	89		37r^1	73[r^1]	83
32v	[62]	89		37v^1	73[v^1]	83
33r	65	139		37r^2	73[r^2]	84
34r	67	212		37v^2	73[v^2]	84
35r	69	160				

[4]   Stephens.
[5]   A. de Vere [3] P.   P.* [7]   pride is madness.
[6]   G. Planche & Barbier

[8]   Gott hat den Menschen einfach gemacht: aber wie er
      gewickelt wird & sich verwickelt, ist sehr† zu sagen.

                                              [1]   M. Arnold
                                                    Ball: Coll:
                                                    1843.

[2]   Rude orator
             Who while I pondered on the lot of Souls
             Born Reason's Heirs, & of that Heritage
             Made void, and held the sorrow & the Joy
             Within the Balance of a slow suspense
             Didst force an audience ere I struck the Scale,
             And dared pronounce them it happy. What are these
             Whereon thou buildest such a goodly Pride
             Thy Proofs thy Witness & thy Precedents
             That they should ease grave Counsel of its Care,
             And win deliberate Reason to put on Fear
             The credulous Complexion of thy Dreams. Woe‡
             —No lack of answer hast thou, o my Heart.
             For such a damning Catalogue of Ills
             Thou dost alledge for Proof, such Instances
             Raked from the swarming Gulfs of Sorrow's Hell,
             And to uphold thy desperate Challenging
             Incitest Reason to forswear her state,
             Make Cession of her sceptre, doom herself
             With such a lavish hardihood of scorn

* Written over erased "To."
† "schwer" intended.
‡ An alternative to "Dreams."

The first page of the Yale Manuscript.

[1843]

[1]   This sheet seems to have originally been the endpaper inside the front cover of a notebook. A. probably wrote this inscription shortly after he purchased the notebook. There is an identical inscription in A.'s copy of *Publii Virgilii Maronis Opera* (London, 1839), now owned by Park Honan, and a similar one for 1844 in the "1847 Notebook" owned by Arnold Whitridge. The date indicates the date of purchase and of the inscription itself.

[1843/44]

[2]   Like all the poems in these pages, this one is untitled. C. B. Tinker and H. F. Lowry called it "Rude Orator" when they first published it in their *Commentary* (1940). A. supplied titles at a relatively late stage of composition and sometimes changed them after publication.

[1846/47]

[3]   "To" has been erased, but it is still clearly discernible. The size of the letters (the largest in the *YMS*) seems to make them inappropriate for anything but a title or some other important heading.
        "P. P." is written over part of the *T* of "To." It is now hemmed in by other entries so that its connection with them, if any, is unclear.

Literary reviews led to entries 4–6. They are bracketed with 7, "pride is madness."

[Apr., 1846/47]

[4]   Playwright George Stephens (1800–1851) published at his own expense two volumes of unproduced poetic *Dramas for the Stage*. In its derisive review of April 18, 1846, the *Spectator* thought the plays sprang from monomania rather than divine

inspiration. (At the time, A. was a regular reader of the *Spectator* [Thomas Arnold (1900), 58].) Two of Stephen's pseudo-Jacobean melodramas, *Nero* and *Self-Glorification*, portray characters driven mad by pride.

[1850]

[5]   The reference to Aubrey De Vere (1814–1902) was probably occasioned by an anonymous review (by Henry Taylor) of *The Waldenses, or The Fall of Rora* (*QR* 72 [1843]: 142–65). Taylor discusses at length De Vere's "A Tale of the Modern Time," the story of a lonely Byronic wanderer whose pride leads to paranoia before he is finally saved by the love of Christ.

If A. came upon this review when he was working on "Empedocles on Etna," as seems likely, he would have paid special attention to Taylor's summary of the central theme of the poem: "to show how formidable an enemy our intellect becomes when, highly cultivated and excited, and yet neither founded in faith nor passionately directed upon any course of external activity, it turns upon the soul. This is, no doubt, a modern state of things; it represents the self-consciousness of the modern imagination, the introverted eye of the modern mind . . ." (158).

In 1843, De Vere published a volume entitled *The Search after Proserpine: Recollections of Greece, and Other Poems*, dedicated to his friend—the reviewer and poet—Henry Taylor. It included an untitled song in two stanzas linking pride and madness ([222]) and another subtitled "Scene in a Madhouse."

[6]   Gustave Planche (1808–57) was "a critic of the very first order," according to A., who considered him second only to Sainte-Beuve among French critics (*CPW*, 3:254; see A.'s letter to Sainte-Beuve, Jan. 28, 1863, in Bonnerot [1947], 532).

A review by Planche appeared in the *RDM*, July 1, 1837, 54–78, under the heading "Poètes et romanciers modernes de la France. XXV. M. Auguste Barbier. *Satires et Poèmes.*"[1]

Auguste Barbier (1805–82) was, like A.'s early favorite Béranger, a political poet and satirist. For a few years poems inspired by the July Revolution of 1830 made him enormously

popular, but his talent and popularity quickly waned, except for
Satires et poèmes, which went through some forty editions. He was
belatedly elected to the French Academy in 1869. According to
his editor, Ch.-M. Garnier, he "was the first great French poet
taking, not exactly English subjects . . . but England herself, and
social aspects of English life, as a theme . . ." (*Iambes et poèmes*
[1907], 127).

Planche praised Barbier's poem on England, *Lazare,* singling
out for special praise the section entitled "Bedlam." In it Barbier
"has sunk his glance to the depth of madness, and under the
tumultuous floods of this terrible enigma he has read, unmis-
takably, the two syllables of the word pride [*orgueil*] . . ." (70).

In *Lazare,* Barbier views London as a vast, dark, infernal city
in which all men arrive at madness. Bedlam becomes not only
the epitome of England, but, ultimately, also the final state of all
mankind—reduced to mere matter or worn out pieces of machinery. For the modern madman "the heavens are empty and
the world a wilderness" ("Bedlam," line 31). ". . . Pride is the
alluring insane path which nowadays leads almost all thought to
mournful idiocy or to blind fury . . ." ("Bedlam," lines 93–95,
revised).

[Feb., 1850/51]

[7]   Probably as an afterthought, A. bracketed the four names in
the upper left-hand corner of the page and added: "pride is
madness." His most likely source for this maxim was Spinoza's
Ethics, part 3, proposition 26n.[2]

François Guizot, in *Pourquoi la révolution d'Angleterre a-t-elle
réussi?* (Paris, 1850), 32, twice referred to in the *YMS,*
also links madness and pride, as does Epictetus, *Discourses*
1.24.71.

A. often found similar ideas in many of the books that attracted him, both ancient and modern.

[8]   "God has made man simple (single, not composite, unfrag-
mented), but how he became wound up and entangled himself
is difficult to say," from a three-sentence letter of Goethe's to

Charlotte von Stein, December 11, 1778.[3] This sentence is preceded by, "Thanks . . . for inquiring about my confusions [mixed-up-nesses]." (Cf. 9r[2], p. 186.)

The references on this sheet show clarity yielding to confusion and youthful self-assurance (especially intellectual and artistic self-assurance) giving way to madness. Several present this development not as an individual aberration but as man's destiny.

NOTES ON DATING

1. This entry, made about the same time that A. was reading Spinoza's *Ethics,* suggests that he read these reviews late in 1850 a date supported by the handwriting. A review by Sainte-Beuve of Mme de Krüdner's (von Krüdener's) *Valérie,* which immediately precedes Planche on Barbier, probably attracted A. to this issue of the *RDM.* In his unpublished diary for 1851, on the page opposite his entry for January 1, A. put *Valérie* on a list of "French books to buy." Barbier is not listed, but A.'s library eventually included the 1837 edition of the book reviewed by Planche.
2. A.'s 1851 diary lists under works to be read in January: the "last three books of Spinosa's *Ethics.*" He read parts 4 and 5 of the *Ethics,* along with some six other books, during the first ten days of January, and quoted from it on four of these days. Because he doesn't mention reading part 3 in January, he probably completed it ahead of schedule, late in 1850. In a letter to Clough of October 23, 1850, A. praised Spinoza's "positive and vivifying atmosphere," noting that he has "been studying [him] lately with profit" (*CL,* 117).
3. A.'s letter of February° 28, 1851, to his sister "K," reveals his familiarity with Goethe's letters to von Stein (*L*). A.'s unpublished diary for 1851 indicates that he did not read these letters in 1851, so it is likely that he read them late the preceding year. The handwriting of this quotation resembles that of "pride is madness." Its placement indicates that it was probably written during the second half of 1850, surely between February, 1850, and February, 1851. (References to this correspondence in A.'s 1852 diary [*N-Bs,* 551–52] apply only to volume 3, not published until 1851. A. owned the three-volume edition of Goethe's letters to Frau von Stein.)

Three stages of composition, revisions made within a year;
not first drafts.

13ᵛ

[1] *1* Night comes—with Night comes Silence, hand in hand—
     2 With Night comes Silence, & with that, Repose:
                drowsy
     3 And pillows on her cold white breast, & locks
     4 Within the marble Prison of her Arms
                rash
     5 The Poet's fond & feverish Melancholy:
                false Breath 2
     6 ~~Freezes~~ the ~~sweet strain~~ on the parted lips,
                —— 1
     7 Cuts short the Feignings of phantastic Grief
                shallow
     8 And steals the ~~honied~~ Music of his Tongue.

[2]   The dropping Patter of a child's small Feet
        Did fall like Rain in the forsaken Street.
                ——

[3]   O monstrous, dead unprofitable world
                        hold
        That thou canst hear, and hearing thy way:
        A voice oracular hath pealed to day—
        To day a Hero's Banner is unfurled.
        Hast thou no Lip for welcome. So I said—
        Man after man, they smiled & passèd on
      A smile of mournful Incredulity
        Each to his Labour. And when all were gone,
          As tho: men spake of life a   Joy
        It chanced, I know not how, my ~~Dream~~ was fled:
        So scornful seemed that smile, so strange, so full
        Of bitter knowledge. Yet the will is free—
        Strong is the Soul & fresh & beautiful—
        The seeds of godlike Power are in us still
        Gods are we—Bards, Saints, Heroes—if we will—
        O barren boast, o joyless Mockery.

64

[Mar., 1844/45]

[1]   Not long after A. composed these lines he included a version
of them in a letter to Clough from Rugby, where he was substituting as an assistant master in the lower fifth form (*CL*, 57).
      The manuscript itself reflects three stages of composition: the
initial surviving version of the poem (V¹), some features of the
letter to Clough (V²), and revisions made after the letter to
Clough (V³). Except for "shallow" (line 8), all revisions seem to
have been made within a year. (The draft of this poem and the
as yet untitled sonnet on Emerson that follows are written with
a care suggesting that they are not first drafts, especially when
compared with the hastily written drafts on the facing page,
14r.)
      Revisions:

      Line 3: "cold white" became "frozen" in V² and "drowsy" in
        V³.
      Line 5: "Poet's" became " 'Usher's' " in V² only; "fond" be-
        came "rash" in V².
      Line 6: "Freezes," canceled by mistake, was restored; "sweet
        strain" became "false Breath" in V³.
      Lines 6 and 7: these lines were reversed in V²; the number-
        ing in the *YMS* indicates A.'s second thoughts.
      Line 8: "honied" became "shallow" in V³.

      Minor changes in V²:

      capitalized "Marble" (4) and "Lips" (6);
      added colons after "comes" (1) and the second "hand" (1);
      replaced "&" by "and" (3);
      replaced "phantastic" by "fantastic" (7);
      added a comma after "Grief" (7).

      The revisions do not reveal any fundamental change in
attitude.

[May, 1844/45]

[2]   A. used the same rhyme reversed for the opening couplet of "A Summer Night." These lines come as close as he ever came to creating imagistic verse, tinged, however, with Arnoldian Romantic pathos and echoes of Tennyson.

[July, 1844/45]

[3]   A. published a revised version of this poem in 1849 under the title, "Written in Emerson's Essays." A.'s copies of Emerson's *Essays* do not contain the poem nor are drafts of similarly titled poems to be found in the volumes to which they refer. The title points not to the location of the original draft but to its subject matter.

    A.'s major debt, however, is to Carlyle rather than to either series of Emerson's *Essays*. What the speaker says in the first six lines, in particular, draws upon Carlyle's preface (v–xiii) to the London edition of Emerson's *Essays* (1841). Many of the key words in A.'s sonnet ("monstrous," "voice," "welcome," "life," "godlike," "mockery") echo the preface with its emphasis on "welcome." Even line 13 owes more to Carlyle's classification of heroes than to Emerson's essay on "Heroism." Arnold, however, took the idea of being a hero from Emerson rather than from Carlyle.

Hastily written drafts and a leaf drawing or doodle.

[1]   What are Man's works
            Whereon he sets most store—his creeping Temples,
            His little fretted Plots of Garden Ground—
            His parcelled Fields—his Gewgaw Palaces—
                                    dear
                  aping   ~~stiff~~ state
                        mocking his own ~~sweet~~
            His puny Parks, mock solemn as himself
                              Skips
            His Trees, all their quaint Tricks & Gambols gone
            Tortured in sullen Clumps & modish Rows
            From the free use of Nature—what are these,
                  mighty   sweet
            The Darling Gods of his dear Workmanship,
            Seen from the diz[z]y Summit of an Alp?

                        ─────────────────

                          monstrous
[2]   To kindle with a ~~mawkish howl~~
                        storm of feignèd Groans
                     March & motion of a
            Or the quick ~~Music of a jingling~~ Rhyme
            The sickly dotage of a dying world—
            Plying the lusty Bellows of my wit
            To keep it's° smouldering Embers half alive

[3]

*Written over "7."

68

[Mar., 1845/46]

[1]   This blank verse attack upon pride (cf. 1r [4–7])—exemplified primarily by the conspicuous consumption and bad taste of the wealthy—depends heavily upon literary stereotypes to express its youthful revulsion.

[2]   Compare line 3 with "Memorial Verses," line 23. The bombast of the attack on man's works barely hides the poet's own frustration.

[3]   The leaf drawing or doodle at the bottom of the page resembles one at the back of A.'s 1845 pocket diary. (His 1846 diary also contains a drawing of leaves, but its configuration is much less like the one on this page.)

[1846/47]

See 1r[3], p. 57.

[Apr., 1846/47]

See 1r[4], p. 57.

[1]   Sacrilege—we kiss
                                    nourish
        Cheeks* that decay to fatten us, and thrive
        Upon our father's' ashes:—Lust;—we grow
        By appetite:—Injustice;—we forgive
        Or punish, and the cross grain'd sentence twists
        Into the avoided Issue: Tyranny—

                                          crown'd†
        Wise men hold back their hand, & fools are ~~bred~~
        For‡ that forbearance: from that hour to them,
        To them reluctant Destiny consigns
        The groaning Nations: from that hour, the chain
        Is rivetted: and History writes down slave
        Against the name of man, and eating wounds
        Widen in the world's heart;—till Misery
        Breeds Wrath, & wrath breed° change, & change, new love.

                        ————

[2]   sich luft machen—[3] gefühl ist alles. [4] τὸ δ'οὖλον &c
[5]   der§ ewige solo

[6]   For while we are, Lucretius, Death is not—
       And when Death is, why we have ceas'd to be—
       So death can touch us never—

* "C" written over "L" [Lips?]. Revisions on this sheet are in pencil, except as noted.
† In ink, as well as the cancellation of "bred."
‡ Written in ink over "Of." Revised after October, 1849/50, because blotted on top of
  an entry of that date on 12v, opposite this page.
§ Written over "dass."

[July, 1847/48]

[1]   Despite the short opening line, this is a kind of blank verse equivalent of the loosely Miltonic sonnets that A. had been writing just a few years before, such as "Written in Emerson's Essays" (13v[3], p. 64) and "Written in Butler's Sermons."

Compared with A.'s earlier poetry, the greater breadth of this poem, and particularly its concern with the fate of nations, is probably owing to his appointment as private secretary to Lord Lansdowne and to revolutionary movements on the Continent. During the preceding year, his reading had included such French historians as Michelet and Bouillé (Allott, "Reading-Lists," 264).

The autobiographical implications latent in the opening lines are all the more obvious because of the Freudian slip involving A.'s uncertainty about whether to use the singular or plural possessive of father. The syntax requires the plural, but A. presumably used the singular and then the plural (without, however, canceling the singular).

The rationalist tradition of eighteenth-century historians— Voltaire, Montesquieu, Gibbon—who pictured the past ironically and at times satirically, left its mark on A. (By contrast, in "Empedocles on Etna," I.ii.121, "Tyranny, pride, and lust" are regarded as abnormal and degenerate.)

[Sept., 1849/50]

[2]   This can best be freely rendered: "make yourself breathing space," room to be yourself and express yourself. In "Empedocles on Etna," A. refers to air—one of the four elements of Empedoclean physics (see 12v[1], p. 128)—and to its metaphorical extensions. As Empedocles reflects both on his isolation from men, particularly as a poet, and on his own stifling self-consciousness, he cries out for "Air! air!" (II.217). Its application to A. appears in a letter to Clough of February 12, 1853: "yes—*congestion of the brain* is what we suffer from—I always feel it and say it—and cry for air like my own Empedocles" (*CL*, 130, and cf. 109, 123). When Empedocles has fi-

nally resolved to die and give himself to the elements, he exults: "The numbing cloud / Mounts off my soul; I feel it, I breathe free" (II.407–8; see also II.272; cf. 5r[2], p. 165).

[3]   "feeling is all": *Werke* 5 (*Faust,* part 1, 3456). These words constitute the core of Faust's reply to Margaret's attempt to achieve assurance that he is a Christian or at least believes in God. Cf. 35r[2] and 5r[3], pp. 160 and 165.

[4]   "but the whole etc.": a reference to lines from Simon Karsten's edition of Empedocles. These words are part of one of A.'s favorite passages, quoted at greater length in 6r[2] (p. 171) and discussed in detail in the commentary for that entry. Having noted the limitations of man's sensory experience, Empedocles observes that, nevertheless, "every man vainly boasts that he has found the whole."

[5]   "the (that) eternal solo." Many years later in a memorial essay on George Sand (1877), A. contrasted her beloved peasant with England's "eternal trio of Barbarians, Philistines, Populace or . . . the eternal solo of Philistinism among our brethren of the United States and the Colonies . . ." (*CPW,* 8:234). "I hate all over-preponderance of single elements," he explained in a letter to his mother of January 21, 1865, "and all my efforts are directed to enlarge and complete us . . ." (*L*; cf. 6r[3], p. 171).

Entries 2–5 all relate to the danger of mistaking a part for the whole and finding in it a satisfactory basis for life. (See again 6r, p. 171, where A. explains his objections somewhat more fully.) A. later continued his attack on one-sidedness, proposing the alternative of culture.

Several years before the preface to *Poems* (1853), which speaks of Faust in terms of doubts and discouragement (*CPW,* 1:1), A. here implies a belief in the inadequacy of romantic self-assertion. He considered the Faust theme, even in the hands of Goethe, "a perilous subject" (unpublished letter to his sister "K," May 11, [1850], in Balliol College Library). In his lectures *On the Study of Celtic Literature,* he insists that Faust is not a glamorously defiant Titan but only a dissatisfied and discontented man (*CPW,* 3:371). Faust's words to

Margaret are an illustration of the folly of single-minded devotion to a life of feeling. "Refusal of [limitation] by the sentiment of love" comes directly after "Empedocles" in A.'s list of topics for poems to be composed in 1849 (25r[5], p. 114). Faust illustrates this false approach to life. The striking words put into the mouth of the narrator of "Tristram and Iseult," III.112–50, make the same point and provide an additional gloss both on *Faust* and on "der ewige solo."

The antithesis to the victims of "this fool passion" (and to the eternal solo or to the proud ones of the Empedoclean fragment) is Sophocles, whose soul was "even-balanced," and "who saw life steadily, and saw it whole . . ." ("To a Friend," lines 9 and 12).

[Mar., 1850/51]

[6]   Except for the reference to Lucretius, this is almost a literal translation (with the order of the clauses altered) of part of a sentence from Epicurus' *Letter to Menoceus,* which A. read in Diogenes Laertius, *Lives of Eminent Philosophers.*[1]

τὸ φρικωδέστατον οὖν τῶν κακῶν ὁ θάνατος οὐθὲν πρὸς ἡμᾶς, ἐπειδή περ ὅταν μὲν ἡμεῖς ὦμεν, ὁ θάνατος οὐ πάρεστιν· ὅταν δ' ὁ θάνατος παρῇ, τόθ' ἡμεῖς οὐκ ἐσμέν.

(10.125)

The Loeb Classical Library translation by R. D. Hicks reads: "Death, therefore, the most awful of evils, is nothing to us, seeing that, when we are, death is not come, and when death is come, we are not."

The address to Lucretius makes clear that these lines were intended for A.'s drama on Lucretius—still in A.'s mind as he worked on "Empedocles"—but the reference to him is nevertheless puzzling. Surely this is not a ghostly Epicurus addressing his disciple more than two hundred years after his own death. If the speech was intended to be put into the mouth of a contemporary of Lucretius, why is Lucretius being informed of a doctrine that is central to his *De Rerum Natura?* (See especially 3:830ff.)

NOTE ON DATING

1. Handwriting combined with external evidence makes clear that A.'s notes on Karsten for "Empedocles on Etna" date from early 1849. Because A. could have found much of the same information in Diogenes Laertius, it is probable that A. did not read his account until after Karsten's. A.'s unpublished diary for 1851 indicates that he read the first six books of Diogenes Laertius in January. There is no subsequent record in any of his diaries of his reading the last four books. He probably began with them, in 1849 or 1850, years for which no diaries have survived. Given his great interest in the Stoics and Epicureans, as well as in Empedocles, it seems reasonable to assume that A. read the last four books first, either immediately after he had finished Karsten or, as seems more likely, late in 1850, and then turned to the first six books. The handwriting of A.'s transcription from Diogenes Laertius of Epicurus' lines on death matches other samples from the last months of 1850. The lines are so close to being a translation that they probably were written immediately after A. read Book 10, which is entirely devoted to Epicurus and his works.

[1]   local govt. as opposed to centralization is a good thing.
—But central official Govt. is better than local *class* Govt.
—It does not develope the capacity & self respect of local
populations: but then neither does a squire Govt. and it saves
from the partiality of these.
—Therefore in England when the question is stated as*
between local and central Govt. it is misleading—the question
is never raised between these: it is in fact between *two forms of
Government from without.*

[2]   —The common run of men have no special gift & can be
applied to anything—All work is for them merely occupation.
Stupid Hobbs who digs turnips would be stupid still if he had
Lord Dulls° library to read

in, and leisure to think in: and so the world loses nothing by
his remaining where he is. And genius is seldom left† digging
in a turnip field without being acknowledged: it has the more
chance of being acknowledged from their° being a large idle
and rich class to be amused by it and to protect it. So under
an aristocracy with all its apparent inequalities, a nation gets
perhaps all the benefit that is to be got out of its members.

[3]   —This is what may be said to show people that the present
state of things is one under which no harm or loss befalls: but
the great argument is that it is inevitable. Take your crust &
be thankful—for if the social fabric be shaken you will lose
even that. And men are very

much attached to their crust, their bird in the hand:—and this
menace does in fact do much to frighten and make them plod

*"is stated as" replaced "arises."
†"left" replaced "found."

24r^2 (cont.)——————————————————————————

on as they are. How many mothers & wives preach throughout England everyday:

the duty of not endangering this crust. What potent auxiliaries
are these to the cause of what is called social order.—Take
care, then, governments that every one has his crust.

24v^2——————————————————————————————

[July, 1847/48]

The argument based upon inevitability is posed as a lesson for government, rather than as A.'s advice. This seems to suggest that perhaps these notes were meant to form the basis for an article (which would have been his first publication in prose). In a letter to his sister "K" from Lansdowne House, March 10, 1848 (in *L*), he writes: "I was myself tempted to attempt some political writing the other day, but in the watches of the night I seemed to feel that in that direction I had some enthusiasm of the head perhaps, but no profound stirring."

[1]   A. remained interested in the role of local government throughout his life. In 1863, he read an article in the *RDM* on centralization and local government in England and France (*N-Bs*, 570 and 629). His first lecture "On the Study of Celtic Literature" (1865) refers ironically to "the glories of our local self-government," in connection with (Anglo-)Saxon Philistinism (*CPW*, 3:295–96). Because the demand for local self-government was one of the central tenets of middle-class liberalism and because in practice it tended to mean class government, A. included it in *Culture and Anarchy* and *Friendship's Garland* as one of the basic elements of Philistinism. "Central official Govt." seems to point toward the idea of a state not governed by class interests but, instead, the embodiment of the collective best self of each class. A.'s interest in this subject continued intermittently to the end of his life. In his last decade, influenced by his experiences on the Continent, he spoke out on behalf of "the extension of municipal organisation throughout the whole country" and of a complementary "system of local [i.e., regional] assemblies" (*CPW*, 9:12 and 10:210).

[2]   Hobbs and Lord Dull are precursors of Zephaniah Diggs and Lord Lumpington (*Friendship's Garland,* letter 6; *CPW*, 5:66ff.; see also 5:403.)

[3]   The Corn Laws were repealed in 1846. A. had recently been taking notes on Edmund Burke's *Correspondence* (1844), which emphasizes how much more dangerous and difficult to eradicate

is a Jacobinism based on "penury and irritation" than one stemming from "fulness of bread" (4:380; quoted in *N-Bs*, 445).
A. never forgot the importance of cheap bread in keeping the
populace pacified (*CPW*, 5:210 and 212). Yet in writing to
Clough following the February Revolution in France, he expressed admiration for "a *whole society* that has resolved no longer
to live by bread alone" (*CL*, 68).

If every one would mend one—

—Well they cry we have mended one: and we must now cry aloud till we mend you & the world.

—I will not ask, are you sure you are mended in this or that particular? but I will ask, are you sufficient for that new, that self contained, abundant life, which we should be mended into. This crusade, this attacking state, is abnormal temporary: it occupies Existence with the same stimulus of noise & outward action, the cowardly self-betaking whereto has been the source of the meanness & blindness of all those you of all those you would mend: are you sure that, with you, beneath the hot outside, reposes a capacity of substantial life?

[Oct., 1847/48]

For additional comments on behavior and self-discipline, see especially $37r^2[7]$, $12v[3]$, $4r[3]$ and [5], and 20r (pp. 84, 128, 195, and 207).

A. took as his point of departure the proverb, "If every man mende one, all shall be mended," which the *OED* traces as far back in English as John Heywood, *Two Hundred Epigrammes, upon Two Hundred Proverbes* (1555). It is the first in the collection and presumably was already proverbial in Heywood's day. "Mend" looks both backwards and forwards, for it means not only restoring to soundness and integrity but also improving and reforming.

A.'s letter to his sister "K" of March 10, 1848, from Lansdowne House (in *L*), suggests the state of mind out of which these observations probably grew. It also makes similar archaic use of the key word *mend*. In *Literature and Dogma* he put similar language into the mouth of Jesus (*CPW*, 6:223).

This page reflects A.'s lifelong distrust of hasty actions, violence, and "the hot outside." In opposition to these anarchic forces, A. later developed the concept of "culture," his vehicle for achieving "a capacity for substantial life." Improvement here stems not from what government does for you but from what you do for yourself.

Lord Lansdowne desires to acknowledge Mr: T. Llewellyn Royd's letter of the 29th inst: /

[Oct., 1847/48]

A. held the post of private secretary to the third marquis of
Lansdowne from April 23, 1847, until he was appointed by
Lord Lansdowne on April 15, 1851, to be one of Her Majesty's inspectors of schools. A. obviously preserved this note because of the comments on the other side of the sheet. It supports
the assumption that many of A.'s reflections were jotted down
during the free time that his position with Lord Lansdowne
liberally supplied. A. tried conscientiously to avoid wasting
stationery.

If a T. Llewellyn Royd (or Boyd) existed, he seems to have
vanished without a trace.

---

[11] The rich may have art as a mere stimulant: it is only for something to do that nous autres pauvres are compelled to regard it otherwise

[1] —The artist has not the same power of passive pleasure from sensuous objects as another, for fear he should enjoy & not *represent*.—

[2] —Translation of this harder Gk: of facts.

[3] —Even aristocracies putting in force social tyrannies avoid appearing to act directly for & from themselves. but put forward the law as an awful necessity behind them & their victims equally—

[4] Cloth'd in the awfulness of unseen Law, Thou thyself, o man, art perhaps to be one of those characters thou hast come across in thy reading,

who *fail*: this wilt thou never understand? thou gazest on the successful as so many manifestations of thyself, & on the unsuccessful as on men who failed to be what thou art: and this, being nothing. Is it that life itself is a present & sensible success, which while thou hast it keeps thee on the level of those who have *wholly existed* not in like case with those who have failed to exist.

---

[5] Les choses arrivent, mais rarement à propos.

---

[6] Meeting a cockney on a Greenwich steamer, instead of laughing, say—does

*"for fear he should" replaced "else he would."

83

this gay unled varmint thing *succeed* with his accoutrements better than I do, or worse.

———

[7] By meditation & observation we attain a faith, & strike one day some good strokes in manners & behaviour: ha, say we, what a power conviction lends to our practice: the next day the nerves are wrong, the manners full of blunder & despicability, and the conviction, metamorphosed into consciousness, riding us like a nightmare. Nor is it true that after repeated failures, we stand.—

[8] —What pure spiritualists, & how unconcerned with cause & effect, have we

been in childhood—like B. Hall, thinking results came by nature.

———

[9] All men have equal rights
            therefore
     All men should have equal enjoyments—
        Oh! A man has *a right* to what he can get—and *then*—why—*necessity is laid upon* him to forego all. He never stands still to make constitutions & Agrarian Laws—But he fills his belly, like the pelican her pouch, and then to his own astonishment, is whipped of Furies to ladle it all out away from himself.

[10] —Epicureanism is Stoical, & there is no theory of life but is.

[Nov., 1847/48]

[1]   The idea that the artist pays a price for his gift is an old one, revived in the romantic myth of the "poète maudit." The romantics often regarded the alienated artist as heroic; A. strips him of glamor and symbolism and points to the cause of the artist's alienation: his need for detachment, even from his own experience.

[2]   "Gk:" Greek.
        When A. speaks of facts in a literary context, he is thinking of anything verifiable by experience. "Facts" are the basic elements of experience and, so, of art. For example, in a letter to his sister "K," he contrasts the "perilous subject" of Faust with the wholesome Greeks, who "are eternally interesting because they have nothing to do with such, but keep nearer to the *facts* of human life" (A.'s italics; unpublished letter of May 11, [1850], in Balliol College Library, Oxford; cf. *CPW*, 1:8). In his inaugural lecture as professor of poetry at Oxford, "On the Modern Element in Literature" (1857), he again singled out "the literature of ancient Greece" as a "mighty agent of intellectual deliverance. . . . It begins when our mind begins to enter into possession of the general ideas which are the law of this vast multitude of facts" (*CPW*, 1:20).

[3]   A.'s attitude toward aristocracies is both more critical and more cynical here than was usual for him at this time. He may be thinking primarily of France, but, as Lansdowne's secretary, he must have observed much that contributed to this disillusioned view of political manipulation.

The remaining passages on this folded sheet touch directly or indirectly upon the nature of success or failure. Even the preceding entries have some bearing on the topic.

[4]   "The awfulness of unseen Law" links this with the previous entry (cf. 32r[1], p. 89). A. argues against confusing merely being alive with genuinely existing (cf. the conclusion of "Lines

written in Kensington Gardens": "Nor let me die / Before I have begun to live"—12r, p. 132). For the theme of success and failure, see unpublished fragment (iii) for "Lucretius" (*P*, 649 and 649n).

[5]   Things occur, but seldom opportunely. A. seems determined not to rely upon chance or good luck, but the implication of this entry is that man lacks control of his destiny.

[6]   Unlike the "blind, led beggar" of "Consolation" (line 29), "this gay unled varmint thing" is "doing as he likes." "Varmint thing" suggests disdain for someone hardly human; yet A. recognizes in the cockney a lower-class version of himself, not only in his gay apparel but also in his clever jauntiness.

[7]   This entry takes as its starting point the Bhagavad Gita. A. writes of it to Clough: "The Indians distinguish between meditation or absorption—and knowledge: and between abandoning practice, and abandoning the fruits of action and all respect thereto. This last is a supreme step, and dilated on throughout the Poem" (*CL*, 71, Mar. 6, 1848; see also 69 and 75). Combining oriental philosophy with English empiricism, A. attempts to achieve faith and conviction as guides to successful living.

Compare his confession to Clough of September 23, 1849: "I have never yet succeeded in any one great occasion in consciously mastering myself . . . at the critical point I am too apt to hoist up the mainsail to the wind and let her drive" (*CL*, 110). In both passages he speaks of the need for faith or prayer and of the delusion that persistence will inevitably lead to success.

[8]   "Cause & effect," to which A. alludes several times in these pages, is his shorthand for the processes operating in the real world. "Spiritualists" who disregard these processes are out of touch with reality and doomed to failure and disappointment. (Cf. "Empedocles on Etna," I.ii.152ff. and 232–41, and 26r, p.209.) The *YMS* is full of A.'s painful attempts to come to terms with man's limitations and with necessity. (See also A.'s contemporary reference to "the high / Uno'erleap'd

Mountains of Necessity" in "[To a Republican Friend, 1848] Continued," lines 6–7.)

The B. Hall referred to could be Bishop Joseph Hall (1574–1656), "our English Seneca," whose Stoicism would have been congenial to A., but Hall always stresses the inadequacy of nature and the need for grace.

It seems more likely, then, that A. is referring to Sir Benjamin Hall (1802–67), for many years the popular M.P. for the parish of St. Marylebone, until he was elevated to the House of Lords as Lord Llanover, in 1859. Big Ben was named for him in recognition of his contributions as first commissioner of public works. Hansard does not record any speech of his in Parliament that could have led to A.'s remark. Perhaps he addressed some fatuous words to the Marylebone vestry, which later repeatedly served A. as an example of Philistinism at its most absurd (*CPW*, 5:28; 1:87; 3:289).

[9]   On a page containing notes on Simon Karsten's edition of Empedocles, A. has written: "Man has an impulse for happiness: he sees something of it, hears traditions of much of it: he thinks therefore he *ought* to have it: what is true is, he *may* have it if he *can*" (Ashley Library A17 1r in the British Library; quoted in *Commentary*, 290n; handwriting suggests a date of 1851—much later than this entry). This early comment contains two important elements not found in the Ashley note: the emphatic reference to right (also italicized in "Empedocles on Etna," I.ii.155, 160) and the emphasis upon necessity, retribution, and restitution. In "Empedocles," the philosopher insists that there are no hostile or malevolent forces (gods or Fate) working against man. Nature is indifferent to him; misfortune comes from the working of natural forces. (Cf. "Lucretius," fragments 3 and 4 in *Commentary*, 346, also in *P*, 649 and 649n.) A. surely recalled Carlyle's rhetorical question in *Sartor Resartus*, "What Act of Legislature was there that *thou* shouldst be Happy?" (*Works*, 1:153).

[10]   This should be read in conjunction with the preceding entry. Because the Epicurean gods are aloof and indifferent to man's

welfare, his happiness depends upon his own efforts. According to the Stoic teaching of Epictetus, man will achieve freedom (and happiness) only by desiring "nothing that belongs to (is in the power of) others" (*Discourses* 4.1.314). A. sees Stoic ethics as the natural outcome of Epicurean theology and believes that no (satisfactory) theory of life can be found that doesn't have at least a Stoical component. But this entry surely was not meant to be the sweeping generalization it appears to be out of context.

A number of commentators understandably regard this final entry on the last sheet of the bound volume as an incomplete sentence. The period, if it is a period and not simply an ink spot, follows "is" at some distance, but that is not unique in these pages.

[11]   This entry is an afterthought, squeezed in at the top of 37r¹. The contrast between the patronizing attitude toward art on the part of the rich and that of "indigent and unfortunate wretches," like A. himself, not only reveals his ironic self-denigration but also his wholesome skepticism about art. Are those who exalt art forced to do so by economic necessity?

A. seems to have written these entries with his drama "Lucretius" in mind.

[1]   If the Laws of the Universe are irrespective of man, the
greater his Gift that he can quietly parcel them out into texts
with a personal application.

[5]   yet we praise
The gay* inventive vein of the blithe† spirit—

[2]   We are not so ill treated if we consider that time and the year
are almost indefinitely prolonged for us in childhood, when
we have always employment for them—& only in fact begin to
hurry when men begin to be pained & puzzled what to do
with them.

[3]   —After all to the behind-Scenes companions of the dissolute
gifted man must genius appear the

most miraculous fact: to distant observers of his happy hours
only, a serene perpetual divine life seems something
wonderful indeed but beautifully possible: while the close-
comers know the delusiveness of this—and yet while they feel
him one of themselves and in a certain Sense an imposture,
are suddenly astonished by jets of light of which in themselves
they know nothing.

[4]   —We learn late the truth of *Cause & effect:* that this or that
operation will bring forth this or that result, & not another:
that a certain merit will not have a *heterogeneous* reward: that
there is no pity—no compromise.—

*Alternative to "blithe."
† Alternative to "free."

[Nov., 1847/48]

[1]   The *YMS* includes many comments upon "the Laws of the Universe," human limitations, and necessity. A. regards the human situation largely in Stoic terms, recognizing the restrictions imposed upon man by the nature of reality. Much of his reading—and especially of Lucretius, in 1848—would have supported this view of man's place in the universe. The word "quietly" suggests both oriental and Stoic influences.

[2]   Because A. is an elegiac poet, it is not surprising to find him at twenty-five looking back nostalgically upon childhood as on a different mode of existence, an attitude reinforced by his reading of Wordsworth. A few years later, he was complaining about the loss of youth, but he already sounds middle-aged.

Although his poems often treat time with great flexibility, he rarely comments directly on man's subjective manipulation of time. "Consolation" comes closest to being explicit in its opposition to man's desire to alter the pace at which time passes.

[3]   A. is unlikely to be thinking of any of his friends in referring to the dissolute genius. Nor is this likely to be a reference to a modern writer (although Burns is a possibility), for A. had not yet become an avid reader of literary biographies. Probably it is an idea for "Lucretius," especially in view of the entry that follows. The mysterious nature of genius was a topic of great interest in the eighteenth century.

[4]   The belief that man must adjust to a deterministic universe indifferent to him is a recurrent theme in the *YMS*. A.'s reading in Lucretius, Epictetus, Spinoza, Goethe, and Burke's *Correspondence* (*N-Bs*, 443) would have supported this position. "Empedocles on Etna," I.ii.221ff. is based upon this philosophical assumption. A page of notes for "Lucretius" includes the following: "the Universe has no pity—impatience." Also included are rough drafts of three stanzas, later revised and incorporated into "Empedocles on Etna," I.ii.397–410 (*Commentary*, 293–94). Notes like these would have helped to shape "Lucretius."

A. regarded the following as a key to the thought of Bishop Butler, whom he had read as a boy and studied at Oxford: "Things and actions are what they are, and the consequences of them will be what they will be; why then should we desire to be deceived?" (*CPW,* 8:12).

[5]　　　　This entry was squeezed in as an afterthought. A. distinguishes between man's individual application of universal laws and a "gay inventive vein." This comment looks as if it had been suggested simply by the preceding one—and it does, indeed, relate to it—but the initial impetus probably came from entry 4, with its comments on cause and effect. (There is no space for anything on this sheet after entry 4.) The "inventive vein" is the product of self-deception; the spirit is not really free but merely living in happy ignorance. Praise of the "blithe spirit" is misdirected because it applauds one who ignores cause and effect, "the Laws of the Universe," instead of coming to terms with them. If A. has in mind Shelley's encomium to the "blithe spirit" in "To a Skylark," this would be one of A.'s earliest attacks upon an aspect of the romantic esthetic. (For another kind of "blithe spirit," see the reference to the cockney on the Greenwich steamer, $37v^1[6]-r^2$, pp. 83–84.) The headnote to "'In Harmony with Nature'" (*P,* 44) helps to illuminate A.'s viewpoint.

And every man relates
The history of his life
So far as he has yet gone:
And we hear him, and perceive not
That his history still lacks
Its unguessed conclusion.

———

And every man has wandered,
    every man wept,
    every man raved
every man buried despondingly in his hands
    His burning brow
    Even as I do:

———

And every man has found a home,
    every man dried his tears,
    every man ceased his ravings:
every man raised cheerfully his head
    Looking forth upon life:
    Shall not I likewise?

———

Here & there are scattered their dwellings:
    On rocks—by rivers,
    In cities—in fields:
Where they have struck root & planted themselves,
    Giving over their wanderings:
Long we wandered they say, but now
    We rest for ever.

Who led you, o men, who ~~planted~~ counselled you
    By this rock, by this river
    In that city, on that field?
Wherefore did you strike root there & planted
                    yourselves:
    Why cease your wanderings?
Long you wandered, I know, but why
    Rest you now here?

——

You know not— you cannot answer:
One by one, over wearied
You dropped down in your wanderings
Where you dropped, there you remained:
You awoke, already rooted & planted there:
  This is the place, you said,
We sought in our wanderings: here
    Rest we for ever.

——

This place, o men, you sought not:
  You chose it not beforehand:
Passing that way in your wanderings
    You dropped down there—
For you alone is it a habitation:
    For you only:
Well is it for you, if you are well there:
    So much I say.—

——

I have not yet dropped down in my wanderings:
    I wander still:
Some time, perhaps I too shall drop down
    In some other city:
Tell me of your wanderings rather: your
      rest for you—your wanderings for all men

[Nov., 1847/48]

These lines touch on two important themes in A.'s poetry: wandering and raving, the latter related to the idea of madness explored in the commentary for 1r[4–7]. Cf. "Rugby Chapel," lines 128–30.

Venus to Juno of Dido & Æneas

[1]   But much I fear, my son will ne'er consent
      Whose armed soul, already on the sea
      Darts forth her light to Lavinia's Shore.

[2]   the storm in the cave.

[3]   I think it was the devil's revelling night
      There was such a hurly burly in the heavens:
      Doubtless Apollo's axle tree is cracked
      Or aged Atlas' shoulder out of joint
      The motion was so over violent.

[4]   Jupiter
      That with thy gloomy hand corrects the heavens
      When airy creatures war amongst themselves.

[5]   Whose golden Fortune, clogg'd with courtly ease
      Cannot ascend to fame's immortal house.

[6]   If he forsake me not, I never die:
      For in his looks I see Eternity:
      And he'll make me immortal with a kiss.

[7]   I hope, that that wᶜʰ love forbids me do
      The rocks & sea gulls will perform at large.

[Dec., 1847/48]

This sheet consists entirely of quotations from *Dido, Queen of Carthage* by Christopher Marlowe (and Thomas Nashe?). A. made very few substantive alterations (noted below). However, he freely altered the punctuation and capitalized "Shore," "Fortune," and "Eternity" in passages 1, 5, and 6 respectively. The heading applies only to the first passage.

[1]   III.ii.82–84. Venus answers Juno's proposal that Venus' son, Aeneas, marry Dido.

[2]   III.iv is headed "A storm. Enter Aeneas and Dido in the cave, at several times." Dido declares her love for Aeneas, who vows to remain and love her forever.

[3]   IV.i.9–13. Aeneas' companion, Achates, speaks to Dido's sister, Anna, and to Iarbas, Dido's royal suitor, about the storm.

[4]   IV.ii.6–7. Iarbas prays to Jove to redress his wrongs. The line reads "Jove" not "Jupiter" in the original, but the character is named Jupiter. A. omitted some words between Jupiter and the rest of the quotation. The original reads "heaven" not "heavens."

[5]   IV.iii.8–9. Aeneas, alone, expresses his desire to leave for Italy to fulfill his destiny.

[6]   IV.iv.121–23. Dido muses to her followers shortly after Aeneas' departure. Dido, who has just made Aeneas king of Carthage, fears he will abandon her for Italy. Aeneas tells her that Mercury bade him leave for Italy at Jove's command. Marlowe later modified the last line to produce the famous address to Helen (*Doctor Faustus*, V.i).

[7]   V.ii.88–89 (or i.170–71). Dido curses Aeneas. The next line is: "And thou shalt perish in the billows' ways." A. follows the early text in using "sea gulls" instead of "sea-gulfs."

For the passages quoted, A. could have used any of the three editions published between 1818 and 1826: Oxberry, Hurst, or Pickering [Robinson]. A. later owned a copy of Dyce's 1858 edition of Marlowe's works.

A.'s preface to *Poems* (1853) and his inaugural lecture "On the Modern Element in Literature" (1857) both express his high regard for the episode of Dido in Virgil's *Aeneid,* upon which the play is based (*CPW,* 1:4, 35. See also "The Scholar-Gipsy," lines 208–9).

The themes of divine opposition to human love and the destructiveness of passion also appear in "Switzerland" and "Tristram and Iseult."

[1]   man is born with a "turn for being a sovereign prince"—&
accordingly this desire, as all his, is stereotyped in the actual &
visible world by the existence of aristocracies &c—to be sure
the individual desirer is often not one of them—but the rule
is saved—let that content him.

[2]   —The poet glances over the throng of orators, men of
business &c and says—how well might this & that man have
been a poet: but the others do not say vice versâ

[1848]

[1]   See the Introduction for A.'s interest in politics and the class
structure.

[2]   This entry may have been meant as an idea for a play. A. was
soon to portray Empedocles: poet, statesman, philosopher, phy-
sician. At the time, A. connected thoughts about the choice of
a career with thoughts about society.

[1]
                                but
                        even while we plan
            Like all his fellows, with a bloody spur
            The breathless moment has shot by, wherein
            We should be what we would be—

[2]   —While we gasp, to wrench ourselves into a mood, and
immediately with that in our clutch, into the general—

[3]   To see this or that hill *once:* rails & a line fence:
we can only *remember* what had *affinity to us.*—

[4]   —While the old man complainingly compares the present with
the past, the young one is experiencing that very delight
which 50 years hence will cause him complainingly to
compare his present with this past. We change & not the
world.

[5]   —is that all my child?—but to ask that is to ask genius.

[1848]

All the entries bear upon the problem of time. Man is a creature swept helplessly along by its destructive force. He is always in flux and a victim of forces beyond his control. As early as "A Question" (ca. 1844), A. had written: "Change doth unknit the tranquil strength of men," line 3.

[1–2] The first entry is a fragment in blank verse, perhaps related to "A Dream" (especially lines 30–33), which uses A.'s favorite metaphor, the river, to express the action of time. "A Memory-Picture" (especially lines 54, 57–58) has even closer likes with this sheet, for it combines the problem of time with the issue of memory, entry 3 below.

[3]   A boyhood memory leads to thoughts about the limitations of memory in general, another illustration of man's victimization by time. In addition to the word "remember," A. underlines "affinity to us," etymologically what borders upon us, largely beyond our control. (See p. 18; cf. letter to "K," Jan. 25, 1851, in L.)

[4]   "Youth's Agitations" presents the same issue from the point of view of a youth who anticipates the reactions of "age" ten years hence. The youth, however, does not consider his situation delightful, although he recognizes that time is likely to make him alter his assessment.

[5]   The child's question is missing, but it seems implicit in what precedes it: "How can I control my own destiny and be what I would be?" A. is telling himself (the child) that he wants what is possible only for a genius.

2 1r¹ _____

[1]   When we have noticed similar phenomena to occur in
      provinces of the natural & spiritual world, we gladly place the
      two operations in juxtaposition: as to do so not only gives a
      livelier sense of the inward operation & graves it clearer on
      the memory: but also awakes in us a pleasurable feeling of
      affinity & correspondence between our selves & nature
      whereof* we never cease to apprehend the existence. But the
      sense of

2 1v¹ _____

      likeness must first strike us: and the facts prove themselves
      & suggest correspondence: while analogists assume
      correspondence, & order us to infer likeness and the *fact*
      of similar† operation in one sphere if they point out
      operation in the other.

2 1r² _____

[2]   We have a will as a refuge to which when weary & despondent
      in following the sinuous recurrent indecisive leading of
      nature, we may betake ourselves & gain therefrom an
      arbitrary definite direction if we will. But those who have a
      strong sense of nature cannot do this with good conscience.

2 1v² _____

*Written over "which."
†"similar" added.

[1848]

[1]   Here "spiritual" refers to the inner world of man. A. is contrasting moral feelings with material phenomena, the mental with the physical, the subjective with the objective.

        For A.'s interest in "affinity," and "correspondence" see the Introduction.

        This cluster of themes—affinity, alienation, memory, the relation between man and nature and between man and his own faculties—is central to the original group of "Switzerland" poems and to "Separation," as well as to those all-embracing poems begun at the end of the forties, "Empedocles on Etna" and "Tristram and Iseult."

[2]   Man's true vocation is to follow nature, however indecisive and sinuous her guidance. (Cf. "Courage," lines 1–2.) To assert one's will gives life a false and arbitrary direction and is an act of bad faith. (See "The World and the Quietist," particularly st. 1, which suggests the influence of the Bhagavad Gita on this observation. See also "Empedocles on Etna," I.ii.221ff. Cf. 4v[1], p. 163.) A.'s comments on the proper way to approach Truth in his preface to *Essays in Criticism* (First Series) reflects a similar outlook, if one substitutes "Nature" for "Truth" (*CPW*, 3:286).

        By Janaury 25, 1851, in a letter to "K," when A. was looking forward to marriage and a possible career as a school inspector, he was vowing to follow the opposite course: using his will to oppose natural affinities that were separating him from her (*L*).

Artistes, harmoniez°

Puisque nulle époque n'est pleinement la contre épreuve
d'une autre époque, nul lieu l'adéquate d'un autre lieu, ne
copiez point les littératures étrangères, etudiez° les seulement:
sachez à fond les procédés a° l'aide desquels elles réalisèrent
au temps de leur spontanéité ce qu'elles sentirent: puis
inspirez vous des circonstances de ce que vous voulez peindre
pour trouver des procédés analogues, aussi sincères, aussi
harmoniques, aussi aptes à produire chez les autres
l'impression par vous sentie.—

[Mar., 1848/49]

"Artists, harmonize. Since no age is the exact counterpart of any other age, and no place the equivalent of another place, do not copy foreign literatures, simply study them: understand thoroughly the processes by which they expressed what they spontaneously felt at the time: then draw inspiration from the circumstances surrounding what you wish to depict in order to find analogous procedures—ones as sincere, harmonious and apt to produce in others the impression you felt." (Source unidentified.)

A. made much use of classical and other foreign literatures, but he turned to them primarily for "excellent" subjects rather than for technique. The chief exceptions were his later attempts in "Sohrab and Rustum" and "Merope" to achieve some of the harmony and simplicity of the Greeks. He discusses the use of models in his preface to *Poems* (1853). One of his later criteria was the "adequacy" of a literature in interpreting its age.

Beethoven. 222.

[1]   Our separation was the necessary result of the instability of
      men's lives, each pursuing his own ends and trying to fulfil
      destiny: the principle of all that is unalterably good still firmly
      uniting us.—

[2]   1_6_2

      I am that which is. I am all that is all that was and all that
      shall be. No mortal man hath my veil uplifted.

[3]   —He is one, self existent and to that one all things owe their
      existence.

[4]   —πάντων μέτρον ἄνθρωπος.

19r²–v² _____

[Mar., 1848/49]

[1]   [Anton Felix Schindler], *The Life of Beethoven,* 2:222, from
        a letter of Beethoven to Dr. F. G. Wegeler, October 7, 1826.
        At this time, and for several years thereafter, A. was acutely
        aware that his nature, ambition, and needs were separating him
        from those who had been closest to him. (See letter to "K,"
        Jan. 25, 1851, in *L,* and *CL,* 95, 109, and esp. 129. Cf. the
        contemporary entry 31r[5], p. 109.)
        The closest parallel is the "Switzerland" sequence, especially
        "Parting," "Isolation. to Marguerite," "To Marguerite—Contin-
        ued," and "A Farewell."
        "Separation," "instability," and the strains resulting from the
        attempt to "fulfil destiny" were all deeply felt concerns at the
        time, as was the conflict between human relations and the pre-
        carious task of finding one's destiny and holding to it.
        The only references to Beethoven in A.'s poetry occur in
        "Epilogue to Lessing's Laocoön," of the mid-sixties, in which the
        speaker's friend places Beethoven with Mozart and Mendelssohn
        as "the kings of sound." The speaker himself gives additional
        emphasis to Beethoven's stature (lines 34–35, 89–A06, 205–
        6) as the preeminent composer who has achieved all that a
        musician can, although falling short of the achievements of po-
        etry, the supreme art.

[2–3]   Schindler, *Life of Beethoven,* 2:163. A facsimile of these in-
        scriptions in Beethoven's handwriting faces 2:162. Bee-
        thoven, Schindler tells us, regarded them as "an epitome of the
        loftiest and purest religion" and kept them framed on his writing
        table. His source was probably Schiller's essay "Die Sendung
        Moses." They are said to be "from the temple of Isis," but en-
        try 3 obviously does not refer to a female divinity. The emphasis
        in the first is pantheistic; in the second, monotheistic.
        Plutarch identifies Isis with Athena in *Moralia* 354C (*Isis
        and Osiris,* sec. 9) and also provides a version of the second in-
        scription. The *Moralia* appears on A.'s reading list at the end of
        his 1845 diary. Bunsen's *Aegyptens Stelle in der Weltgeschichte,*
        which A. read in 1845, also quotes the passage from Plutarch
        (Allott, "Reading-Lists," 260, 262).

A. twice drew on his memory of the Isis image: in "Maurice de Guérin" and, obliquely, in his preface to *Essays in Criticism, First Series* (*CPW*, 3:34 and 286).

The dating of this page by means of handwriting analysis seems to be supported by the rare reference to Beethoven in a letter to Clough of May 24, 1848 (*CL*, 81).

[4]   "Man is the measure of all"—attributed to the agnostic sophist Protagoras (ca. 485–415 B.C.), usually in the form, "man is the measure of all things," twice quoted by Plato, in *Cratylus* 386A, and in *Theaetetus* 152A.
         A. probably accepted Goethe's interpretation of this gnomic utterance: "We may watch nature, measure her, reckon her, weigh her, etc., as we will. It is yet but our measure and weight, since man is the measure of things" (*Conversations with Riemer*, Aug. 2, 1807, cited in Gomperz, *Greek Thinkers*, 1:451: *Werke*, 22:469). In his essay on "Heinrich Heine," A. commends Goethe for putting "the standard, once for all, inside every man instead of outside him" (*CPW*, 3:110). On this page A. juxtaposes the world seen from the point of view of man with that from the point of view of God. This is the context, too, of the imagined address to the gods that Empedocles puts in the mouth of man (I.ii.339–41). But man is mistaken, says Empedocles (essentially agreeing with Protagoras), for there are no gods who possess vision or standards superior to man's (cf. 6r[2], p. 171).

The entries on this page form a dialectic from which A. probably hoped a synthesis would emerge.

[1]   For Plato says—knowledge is Memory—
       Which is by gracious children gladly tasked
       But grosser subjects ask necessity.

---

[2]   Thought is ours to think ⎱ truly with
       Speech is ours to speak ⎰   endless).

[3a] We would mould & educate as if our wish could change the
[3b] reality: as if in deference to the Protestant Parent's feelings
       Nature would keep out of his childs° sight all but the
       Protestant aspect* of the Universe.

---

[4]   Think what we like—delusion after delusion—there are
       enough of them to last our life through—

---

[5]   When shall we learn that it is our weakness not our
       superiority that hinders our

feeling with every man & action we come across.

---

[6]   —We can represent speakers of whom the sentiments are in
logical sequence both in the monologue and the dialogue—
but this gives us exactly the most generalised abstract sketch
of man, which is a thing of the understanding's shaping, not
in nature—nay which nature abhors.—We can represent man
"acting in speech" generally with logical sequence, & now &
then shewing the characteristic: this is Goethe's faithfulness to
Nature: Shakspeare developes the man throughout from his
characteristic, & holds him always above the general &
characterless—hence his real but unapparent faithfulness.

*"aspect" replaced "segment."

[Mar., 1848/49]

[1]   Written in black verse.

Plato: "if this knowledge which we acquired before birth was lost by us at birth, and if afterwards by the use of the senses we recovered what we previously knew, will not the process which we call learning be a recovering of knowledge . . . termed recollection?" (*Phaedo* 75E; *Dialogues,* 1:429.) Plato, however, distinguishes between recollection and memory. Recollection is the revival or recovery of consciousness, while memory is the preservation of consciousness or knowledge (*Philebus* 34; *Dialogues,* 3:588f.). A. read widely in Plato during 1845–46 (Allott, "Reading-Lists," 257–62).

A.'s wry application of Plato's dictum to elementary education—a strange foreshadowing of his experience as school inspector—has important implications for all men. Only the elect (elite) are truly studious, because they enjoy the pursuit of knowledge (recollection). (Ironically, Dr. Arnold would have considered his son one of the "grosser subjects.")

[2]   What A. probably has in mind here is Plato's belief that thought and speech are not given to man to use indiscriminately but are intended to help him in the pursuit of Truth. Since Truth is one of Plato's infinitely remote Ideas or Forms, its pursuit is endless.

[3]   Far narrower in outlook than Platonism, modern Protestantism, A. believed, ignores the reality principle, the fact that man is subject to necessity.

[3a]   A. insists once more that man must adjust to reality, instead of expecting the world to take directions from him. (Cf. "Empedocles on Etna," I.ii.182–86, 221.)

[3b]   This passage foreshadows part of A.'s attack upon Protestant Dissent, which he considers inadequate because it fails to respond to all that Nature has to offer.

[4]   Platonic Truth, even truth with a small *t*, evades our grasp. Senancour in *Obermann* pictures man as one "who, drifting from illusion to illusion, . . . never does more than dream of life" (Letter 71; Barnes, 2:149; Michaut, 2:137). Behind both A. and Senancour may be the Indian doctrine of *māyā:* "The world as a universal lure, in which man is flung from deception to deception" (cited in Sells, *Matthew Arnold and France*, 77).

[5]   Weakness kept A. from remaining aloof from old friends (*CL*, 95, 129; see also his letter to "K," Jan. 25, 1851, in *L*). Among the materials for "Lucretius" is this note (ca. 1849): "to be weak is to be miserable" (*Commentary*, 293). Cf. 4r[3], p. 195.

[6]   A. is beginning to think seriously about the art of playwriting. Shakespeare's superiority is the result of his presenting the inner character as a *gestalt* rather than as an assemblage of individual characteristics. "[A]cting in speech" seems to be his recollection of Goethe's partial definition of drama in "Shakespeare und Kein Ende" as "Gespräch in Handlungen" (conversation in action)—*Werke*, 14:765. (Cf. 36v[2], p. 112.) The phrase occurs in a paragraph that distinguishes between drama and dialogue. On the same page, Goethe says of Shakespeare that "by his treatment, his *revelation of the inner life*, he wins the reader" (Spingarn, 185; emphasis added). This is what A. meant by Goethe's emphasis upon "the characteristic" in art.

    In a letter to Clough, A. remarked: "You might write a speech in Phèdre—Phedra loquitur—but you could not write Phèdre" (*CL*, 81).

[1] after all why am I restless because I have no one to say with
     tearful eyes to—I am wretched—& to be answered by—mon
     pauvre enfant—allons—sortons—dinons—&c ⟨sketch⟩   &c—.

[2] —Could we *imagine* a character we could be it—but we can
     only hope it: this is a bastard imagination: yet do young
     Geniuses thrive on it & its warmth, or on its absence & the
     liveliness of the constructive faculty?

[May, 1848/49]

[1] "my poor boy—come—let's go out—let's dine—"
This reference to a French-speaking young woman who is no longer around to comfort A. seems to point to the Marguerite of his "Switzerland" poems. The sketch of a woman's head in profile—alas, not very detailed—reinforces the hypothesis that he had a specific woman in mind. All one can say is that she wears her hair up in curls and seems no more cheerful than the artist who drew her. If A. met and flirted with "Marguerite" at Thun, in September, 1848, the entry would have been made not long after. According to the poems, A. and Marguerite met again the following September, but the parting then was less amicable. (Cf. Park Honan's identification of "Marguerite" as Mary Claude, a neighbor in the Lake District, who failed to meet A. at Thun. Honan reproduces this page with its sketch [Honan, facing 290].)
Restlessness is one of A.'s favorite poetic themes. In "A Farewell," lines 17–20, A. ascribes it to Marguerite herself.

[2] The letter s in the word bastard has been crossed out, apparently an attempt by someone to bowdlerize the manuscript. The cancellation does not resemble A.'s own method of canceling words.
Art and life overlap in this entry. Cf. R. W. Emerson, "The Poet": Imagination "is a very high sort of seeing, which does not come by study, but by the intellect being where and what it sees . . ." (Essays [1844], 17).
Imagination requires total identification or empathy. On the other hand, hope—bastard imagination—apes appearances. One leads to possession, the other to the hope of possession; one is actual, the other potential. Without hope, young would-be geniuses rely upon "the liveliness of the constructive faculty" or fancy, rather than upon Coleridgean imagination.

[1]   <u>Comp—1849.</u>

[2] chew Lucretius.

[3] compose:

[4] Empedocles—refusal of limitation by the religious sentiment

[5] Eugenia—refusal of d[itt]o by the sentiment of love
                                                    gleaning

[6] To Antonia—a system of the Universe.

[7] To Meta—the cloister & life liveable

[8] Kantire & the net driers

[9] Thun & vividness of sight & memory compared: sight would
     be less precious if memory could equally realize for us.

[10] An Eastern court—dancing—consciousness—one bayadère
     appearing behind the other.

[11] Shelley—Spezzia—Ah an eternal grief. The Alexandrian
     pessimism.

[12] Narcissus—some wish to be thy lover.

              [13]   [14]   [15]
     5 sonnets—outthunder—So far—When I have

           [16]
     found.—It may be true that men *cannot* do the best they can
           [17]
     devise: it is equally true they *have* never yet done it.—5—

[18] —religious yearning—an education by a chapel—youth—
     marriage—children—death
     the religious longing never quenched.

[19] The first mesmerist.

[20] The bête northern invaders turnd back by the iron shoe trick.

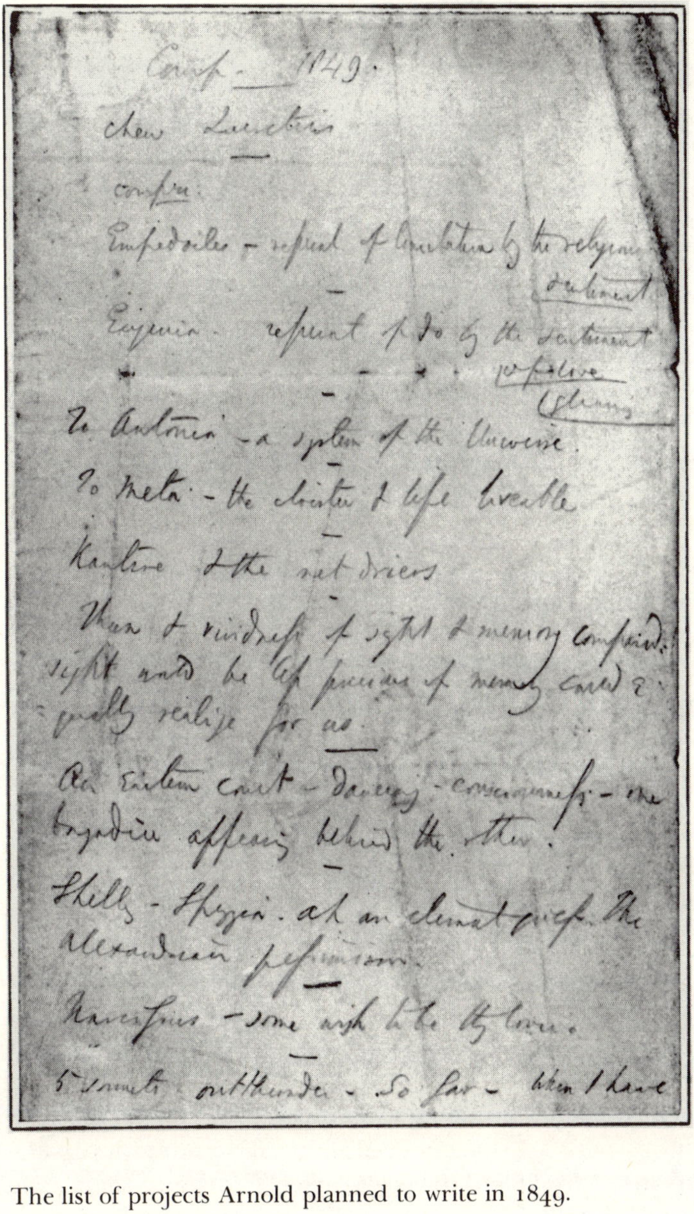

The list of projects Arnold planned to write in 1849.

[Oct., 1848/Jan., 1849]

This sheet can be dated more precisely than any other because of
entry 9, the basis for "To my Friends, who ridiculed a tender Leave-
taking." The limits are set by A.'s first visit to Thun in September,
1848, and the publication of the poem on February 26, 1849, in
The Strayed Reveller, and Other Poems.

[1]   "Comp[ose]—1849." For the poems A. completed in 1849, see
        P, 113–238, to which should be added "Lines written in Ken-
        sington Gardens" (11v–12r, pp. 131–32) and probably a few
        others. For a discussion of the differences between what A. planned
        to write in 1849 and what he actually wrote, see pp. 30–31 and
        the comments following the notes on entry 20 below.

[2]   To "chew" is to ruminate mentally. "Lucretius" heads the list
        because A. viewed it as his largest and most important project.
        "Chew" shows that he realized that it was a long-range under-
        taking. In March, 1849, A. was hoping to complete it in
        1851. The *YMS* contains some of the earliest surviving prod-
        ucts of his work and the *Commentary* (293) reproduces some
        from late 1848/49.

[3]   The word is probably "compose," but it may be "compare."
        Compose seems redundant in view of the first line, but the fact
        that it comes after "chew" may indicate A.'s wish to distinguish
        between "Lucretius" and works he intended to complete during
        the year. If the word is "compare," then A. meant to set up a
        pair of companion poems, entries 4 and 5, illustrating different
        forms of "refusal of limitation." Surely neither poem, then, was
        to be lengthy.

[4]   When A. made this list, he was probably thinking in terms of
        a poem of perhaps two hundred or three hundred lines, like
        "Resignation" or "The Strayed Reveller." Not until some time
        between March and June, 1849, did "Empedocles on Etna" start
        to become a long dramatic poem and supplant "Lucretius" as
        his current major project. (In June, J. C. Shairp read enough of

"Empedocles," probably I.ii, to realize that A. was launched on a large-scale work—Clough, *Correspondence*, 1:270.)

Empedocles' refusal to be limited by the religious sentiment is hardly more than a minor facet of the poem A. wrote. The refusal figures in Empedocles' homily to Pausanias, I.ii, but is not a serious problem for Empedocles himself. The beginning of the entry on 27r[1] (p. 137) is more explicit about Empedocles' rejection of "religious consolations" than is the poem itself.

[5]   Probably never written. Eugenia appears in two of A.'s poems, "Horatian Echo" (1847) and "Philomela" (1852/53?).

"[G]leaning" may refer to the intuitive approach to experience involved in a poem about love and its limitations. (Cf. "To Meta," line 36 (28v, p. 123) and "The New Sirens," lines 79–80, where the heart gleans from the Gods more "than the toiling head.") On the other hand, "gleaning" may mean that A. planned to use some fragments of an unsatisfactory poem (which he did not offer for publication until 1887) in a new and better poem. As it stands, "Horatian Echo" has little or nothing to do with "refusal of [limitation] by the sentiment of love."

[6]   Probably never written. "Lucretius" and then "Empedocles" absorbed A.'s interest in large philosophical questions. He was concerned about finding a controlling vision, an "Idea of the world," but he tended to be scornful of systems and system makers. A. later ironically characterized himself as "a plain, unsystematic writer without a philosophy" (*CPW*, 5:137).

[7]   For "To Meta," see 28r–v and the commentary on 28 r–v, pages 122–24.

[8]   Probably never written. Kantire maybe an anglicization of Kantier, which, according to Lorédan Larchey, *Dictionnaire des noms* (1880), is the Breton form of Cantié (or Cantier), and is related to "vannier," a basket maker. Perhaps A. had some Breton folktale or ballad in mind. His library contained two volumes devoted entirely to Breton popular songs and to Breton bards, published during the sixties by le Comte de la Villemarqué.

"Tristram and Iseult" and "Stanzas from Carnac" also attest to his deep-seated interest in Celtic Brittany.

[9]   This points toward "To my Friends, who ridiculed a tender Leave-taking" (appropriately retitled "A Memory-Picture," in 1869). It was probably the first poem in which A. refers to Marguerite. From 1853–69 it began the "Switzerland" sequence of poems; then, in 1877, he relegated it to a place among his "Early Poems."

[10]   Probably never written. Presumably, this poem was to be like "Mycerinus" or the later "Sohrab and Rustum"—poems with exotic oriental backgrounds that deal with timeless moral issues. "Consciousness" seems out of place in A.'s entry, but he must have intended it as the major thematic force behind the poem (again, like "Mycerinus"). Concern with consciousness, like so much else, became absorbed into "Empedocles" (see, for example, II.345–54). Later *spontaneity of consciousness* became central to A.'s concept of Hellenism (*CPW*, 5:165 and passim).
        The bayadères were Indian temple dancers, often prostitutes. Goethe wrote a poem entitled "Der Gott und die Bajadere. Indische Legend" (*Werke*, 1:158–60). A popular French romantic ballet-opera of 1830 with the same title was choreographed by F. Taglioni, to music by Daniel Auber and a text by Eugène Scribe. A. probably read the article by Émile Montégut, "Les symptômes du temps, III," in *RDM*, July 1, 1848, 109, which refers to "bayadères aux danses lascives." Montégut draws up a series of oppositions that include the bayadères, on the one hand, and austere penitents, on the other.

[11]   As C. B. Tinker points out in his article on this sheet and in *Commentary*, 253, this entry (or rather, the first sentence of it) underwent a marked contraction to become the basis for lines 139–44 of "Stanzas from the Grande Chartreuse," probably not written for several years. There is grief in the lines, but it is only transitory. A contemporary poem, "Dover Beach," *is* concerned with "The eternal note of sadness" (line 14) and with the more or less permanent state of "human misery" (line 18).

(Earlier, in "Obermann," A. had written of the "ground-tone / Of human agony" [lines 35–36].)

"The Alexandrian pessimism" plays no discernible role in the lines A. wrote. The pessimism, again, was probably drained off into "Empedocles." But why Alexandrian? Alexandria was noted for its Neoplatonic school and that supplies a link with Shelley, a confirmed Platonist and Neoplatonist, but Alexandrian traditions were anything but pessimistic. But perhaps A. recalled Proclus (ca. 410–85), in the lectures of Victor Cousin, *Cours de l'histoire de la philosophie,* read in 1845 (Allott, "Reading-Lists," 259–60). Proclus, the last major Greek philosopher, is considered an Athenian, having headed the school of Plato in Athens. Cousin calls him "the Aristotle of Alexandrian mysticism" (probably a reference to his influence there), ending "in mystic hymns, coloured with a profound melancholy, in which it may be seen that he despairs of the world..." (lecture 8, Cousin [1829], 1:330; translated by Wight in Cousin [1852], 1:386).

[12]   Probably never written. Narcissus usually symbolizes self-love and introspective self-contemplation. His lovers are doomed to frustration. None appear in A.'s poetry, but the "Switzerland" poems speak of the torments of lovers for whom communication is impossible, and there is a narcissistic side to "Obermann," without the selfishness.

[13–15]   These laconic references point toward poems already begun, for they are too lacking in specificity to suggest subjects for poems.

"So far": the opening words of the sonnet "The World's Triumphs" (published in 1852 as "Sonnet"). Tinker and Lowry are probably right in seeing "When I have found" as a reference to "Youth's Agitations" (also simply called "Sonnet," in 1852), which now begins "When I shall be divorc'd..." and which, in 1869, A. placed next to "The World's Triumphs." Both use the Shakespearean sonnet form and so stand apart from A.'s other sonnets (including "Shakespeare").

"[O]utthunder" is probably a reference to the draft of a sonnet or part of one that he discarded, perhaps in the bombastic style of some of A.'s earliest poems in the *YMS.*

[16–17]   Concern about the gap between conception and expression or execution is a common theme in these pages. See 5v[1] and 3r[1], pp. 168 and 154. The idea that imagination outstrips performance is in part what lies behind A.'s lifelong championing and pursuit of perfection. See 2or, p. 207.

[18]   Probably never written. A. may have used the central elements for "Tristram and Iseult." "To Meta" and "Stanzas from the Grande Chartreuse" involve religious yearning.

The placement of this entry near the bottom of the list may indicate that, like the next entry, it was a topic for a poem he did not expect to begin soon. "The religious longing never quenched" describes A.'s own position. His reading and writing were ways of sublimating that longing.

[19]   This ultimately led to "The Scholar-Gipsy" in 1852–53. C. B. Tinker's discussions of this sheet in his article and in *Commentary*, 205ff., explore the link between mesmerism and Joseph Glanvill's *The Vanity of Dogmatizing* and note that A.'s mother shared an interest in mesmerism with their Fox How neighbor Harriet Martineau. (See also *P*, 355–57.) A. never totally abandoned the idea of mesmerism. It accounts for the Scholar-Gipsy's search for the power to bind men's thoughts. A. did not begin serious work on the poem until at least 1852, as the listing of "the wandering mesmerist," under poems for 1852, indicates (*Commentary*, 17). The introduction of the theme of wandering was an important step forward in the conception of the poem, but even as late as 1851, A. was still apparently giving mesmerism a large role in the poem, but by then it may have simply become a code word for the poem itself.

[20]   Probably never written. This refers to a tale from the *Saga of Ragnar Lodbrok* (*Commentary*, 13).

Except for "Lucretius," this list of projects was probably intended as a plan for a volume of poems to be published within a year or so. Aside from two sonnets, which must already have been at least partly drafted, A. published only four other items on the list: entries 4, 9,

11, and 19—entry 4 much expanded and 11 greatly contracted. "The first mesmerist" became, in "The Scholar-Gipsy," very different from what he must have had in mind here, and work on it did not begin in earnest for three or four years. Only one poem written in 1849, entry 9, came at all close to his original conception, and that poem is more about time and memory than about sight and memory. Perhaps as many as ten of the eighteen projects were never even begun, vanished without a trace, or were metamorphosed into totally different poems. See pp. 30–31.

Calm'd by bitter disabusings
   Of all thirst of earthly things—
Ah! they walk in starry musings
   Like Stone-sculptu[r]d antique kings—
5 Slowly, past the open spaces
   Of their Cloister, see, they glide—
Tears have washed those austere faces—
   Neither hate have they—nor fear—nor pride.

   See, one figure quits the mazes
10 Of that dusk slow-moving band,
This way moves, & pauses, gazing
   On the sweet and moon bathed land:
Softly gleam the far blue mountains:—
   Dark* the valley sleeps in shade
   Cool
15 Calm, the murmur of the fountains
                   charmd
   Sinks & rises thro: this cool arcade.

Here, where life & all things living
   Awe-struck fain would cease to be,
Meta, with a vague misgiving
20 Your sweet eyes are turnd on me:
Where, you whisper, is assurance
   Of a spirit softly clear
   Of calm wishes, mild endurance—
   All the heart enjoins, but only here?

———

*Written over "Calm."

25 Spare me, Meta! Question rather
  That lone gazer leaning near—
 Touch his robe & say—My father,
 Tell me, is it quiet here?
Say, my father, does the tired
30 Restless heart, in this retreat
Learn to know what it desired,
 Knowing clasp it, & securely beat?

_____

At your voice he rises slowly
 From the pillar where he leans—
35 In your gentle melancholy
 All you[r] spirits° history gleans:
Scans those parted lips, that purely
 pleading gaze—that forehead clear—
 Signs the cross and answers, surely
40 You say true my daughter, peace is here.

_____

[Oct., 1848/Apr., 1849. Winter 1849, most likely.]

C. B. Tinker christened the poem "To Meta: the Cloister and Life Liveable," when he published it in an article on "Arnold's Poetic Plans," *YR* (1933), basing his title on A.'s *YMS* list.[1] Kenneth Allott's briefer title, "To Meta," seems more in keeping with A.'s own practice. This is one of several poems A. planned dealing with constraints upon man's life; here, the limitations imposed "by the cloistered or regular life" (*Commentary*, 338).

A. may have based Meta upon his sister "K," the model for the Fausta of "Resignation" (*Commentary*, 339), but Meta seems vaguer, less restless, and more melancholy. Park Honan suggests Mary Claude as the model (Honan, 158ff.). Meta seems to embody an aspect of A. himself, and she asks questions that he was asking. This does not rule out a female model as well. The correspondence with Clough shows how A. could warn another against the dangers he felt threatening himself. The poem externalizes the internal dialogue.

Lines 3–4: The allusion is to bas-reliefs on the Black Obelisk (ca. 841–824 B.C.) of Shalmaneser III, king of Assyria (858–824 B.C.), found at Nimrud by Austen Henry Layard.* When the obelisk arrived at the British Museum in October, 1848, thousands flocked to see it and in December detailed drawings of it appeared in the *Illustrated London News*.

Line 11: "gazing"—a slip of the pen. The rhyme requires "gazes." The slip suggests that this is not A.'s first draft. It contains few revisions.

The poem has much in common with "Resignation" and also more obviously with "Stanzas from the Grande Chartreuse." Except for the last line, A. adopts the eight-line trochaic tetrameter stanza of "The New Sirens."

---

*The obelisk celebrates military victories (most notably over King Jehu of Israel), but A.'s contemporaries put it in a religious context, because it pictures Assyrians acting under the aegis of heavenly bodies and even more because it seems to support Old Testament history. (Cf. the reference to a runic stone in "Stanzas from the Grande Chartreuse," line 83.)

Layard's account of his most celebrated discovery in *Nineveh and its Remains* was hailed by the *Times* as "the most extraordinary work of the present age" (Feb. 9, 1849, 5).

NOTE ON DATING

1. The dating is based upon the following evidence:
    1. The appearance of the topic "To Meta—the cloister & life liveable" on the list of topics headed "Comp.—1849," which cannot have been drawn up before October, 1848 (see commentary on 25r–v, p. 116).
    2. The allusion to "Stone-sculptu[r]d antique kings" (discussed at lines 3–4).
    3. The handwriting, which supports points 1 and 2 and suggests the terminal date of April, 1849.

1 And that golden fruited strand
2 Near where Atlas hath his stand
3 Bearing on his shoulders broad
4 Earth, & Heaven's star-spangled load,
5 In the farthest western wild
   There or
6 Or far eastward, where uppil'd
7 To maintain the Caspian free
      tyranous° fiercer
8 From the encroaching Euxine sea
   snowy wintery
9 In his* ~~roseate~~ light austere
10 Great Elborus whitens clear:
     rifted
11 Prisoning in his crevic'd Stones
12 The too-daring Titan's bones

*Written over "her."

[Sept., 1848/49. Jan./Apr., 1849, most likely.]

Tinker and Lowry (*Commentary,* 337–38) gave it the title "The Pillars of the Universe." A. probably wrote it shortly after taking notes on Karsten late in 1848 or early in 1849 (Ashley Library A17). The date is based upon the most likely period for early work on "Empedocles on Etna" and upon calligraphy.

Line 1: Refers to the Garden of the Hesperides, where Hera placed the golden apples given her by Ge (Earth) at her marriage to Zeus. A. combines two senses of the word *strand*—a faraway country and a land bordering on the sea or ocean. One of the labors of Hercules was to obtain the apples guarded by the Hesperides and the dragon Ladon. (See "Fragment of an 'Antigone,' " 90–92.) In some versions Prometheus advised Hercules to seek the assistance of Atlas.

Line 2: Atlas—son of the Titan Iapetus and brother of Prometheus. For his opposition, Zeus sentenced him to bear heaven and earth upon his shoulders. The Atlas mountains of Morocco take their name from the myth. (In "Heine's Grave," England replaces Atlas, lines 87–96.)

Line 3: "the farthest western wild"—near the Pillars of Hercules, the western boundary of the ancient world.

Line 8: Euxine—Black Sea.

Line 10: Elborus—the highest peak (18,481 ft.) of the Caucasus and of Europe (if the present Georgian Soviet Socialist Republic is considered to be in Europe).

Lines 11–12: For rescuing man from ignorance by stealing fire from Olympus and for teaching man the arts and sciences (and for other reasons), Zeus condemned Prometheus to be chained to the Caucasus and to have his liver perpetually eaten by an eagle. (See also notes on lines 1 and 2 above.)

This may have been intended to be one of Callicles' songs in "Empedocles on Etna" and represents a very early stage of A.'s work on the poem. The Atlas and Caucasus mountains would have provided an appropriate frame for a poem focused on Mt. Etna. In myth, all three attest to Zeus' irresistible power—over Atlas, Prometheus, and Typho, the fire-breathing monster buried under Etna ("Empedocles on Etna," II.37ff.).

[1]   *1* Τέσσαρα τῶν πάντων ριζώματα πρῶτον ἄκουε·
  2 πῦρ καὶ ὕδωρ καὶ γαῖαν ἰδ᾽ αἰθέρος ἄπλετον ὕψος·
  3 ἐκ γὰρ τῶν ὅσα τ᾽ ἦν, ὅσα τ᾽ ἔσσεται, ὅσσα τ᾽ ἔασιν.

fire—water—earth & the immense height of air.

[2]   —only in a nation where certain thoughts & feelings are new—not common to the bulk of the nation but arising in one man, do they come to a great literary expression. The thoughts & feelings of Goethe were those of an Englishman or Frenchman born in a nation of Germans—hence their retentissement. In a country where everyone has them they are treated as subjective lumber. Yet how much is thus lost

[3]   —our concerning ourselves with other men ought only to* be a result of our world-insight & objective prudence—& must not be confounded with our duty of self discipline & self cultivation.

*"ought only to" replaced "can only."

[Sept., 1848/49]

[1]   Dated by the writing in English, on the assumption that the
        quotation and the English translation of line 2 were made at
        about the same time.
            Verses 74–76 of Empedocles' ΠΕΡΙ ΦΥΣΕΩΣ (On Nature),
        Karsten, 2:96.

        Quatuor rerum omnium radices primum audi:
        ignem et aquam terramque immensumque aethera:
        ex his enim orta, quaecumque sunt et fuerunt eruntque.
                            (Karsten's Latin trans., 2:97)

        Hear first the four roots of all things:
        fire and water and earth and the immense height of air:
        for arisen from these, come all that are and have been and
            shall be.
                            (Based upon K. Allott's trans., P, 187n.)

            A.'s quotation is accurate except for the omission of the rough
        breathing mark over the initial ῥ in line 1. Karsten places the
        lines in parentheses because they are essentially a repetition of
        lines found separately elsewhere in the poem (verses 55,
        105, and 132). See Karsten's explanation, 2:189. (Hermann
        Diels thus omits this passage from his definitive *Die Fragmente
        der Vorsokratiker.*) The source of the lines is Clement of Alexan-
        dria, *Stromata* (ca. A.D. 200), book 6, chapter 2, devoted to Greek
        plagiarism. The lines are said to be taken from a certain Atha-
        mas the Pythagorean.
            A. makes use of the four elements in "Empedocles on Etna,"
        act 2, especially lines 331–44. The belief in ultimate ele-
        ments also lies behind Empedocles' remarks on reincarnation.
        (See P, 201–2n for Karsten on reincarnation.)

[Oct., 1849/50]

[2]   "retentissement": reverberation.
            "subjective lumber": a useless burden, because instead of sup-
        plying what is new and fresh and therefore assumed to be use-

ful, it echoes what is in the air and so is simply an expression of the national *Zeitgeist*.

These comments were probably occasioned in part by A.'s reading of Heine's *Reisebilder* (*Travel Pictures*) and Goethe's *Aus meinem Leben: Dichtung und Wahrheit* (*Poetry and Truth from My Life*), especially book 7. Both reveal the significant influence of society upon writers. A.'s letters at this time comment on the differences between national literatures. (See letter to his mother, May 7, 1849°, in *L*, and note its connection with his reading of the biographies mentioned in his next letter, July 29, 1849. See also *CL*, 142–43, and commentary on 7v, p. 200.)

A. completely altered his position later, most notably in "The Function of Criticism at the Present Time" (1864), by which time A.'s concerns were no longer those of a struggling young poet (*CPW*, 3:262–63).

[3]   Only the need to see life as a whole, to embrace the All, and to develop an "Idea of the world" should lead us to "concern . . . ourselves with other men." Self-discipline and self-cultivation, on the other hand, require detachment from the distractions of society. (Cf. *CL*, 110–11.) Two decades later, A. had come to see how interrelated are self-cultivation and the welfare of other men (*CPW*, 5:112).

1:1   In this lone open glade I lie
2:2   Screen'd by dark trees on either hand:
3:3   And at its head, to stay the eye,
4:4   Those dark-topp'd red-bol'd pinetrees stand

—

5   The clouded sky is still & grey—
6   Thro: silken rifts soft winks the sun:
7   Light the clear foliaged chestnuts play:
8   The massier elms stand grave & dun.†

—

9:9   That child who darts across the glade
10:10   Drags to his nurse his broken toy:
11:11   The brown thrush crosses overhead
12:12   Deep in her unknown day's employ.

—

13:13   Here where I lie what marvels pass
                 active
14:14   What swarming endless life is here:
15:15   Buttercups ~~da~~ clover, daisies grass,
16:16   An air-stirr'd forest, fresh & clear.

—

17:17   Not fresher is the mountain sod
                 lone
18:18   Where the tired angler lies, stretch'd out,
19:19   And eas'd of basket & of rod
20:20   Counts his day's spoil, the spotted trout

—

         Yet here is peace for ever new
       Yet
21:29   But here this calm is nothing new:
22:30   When I who watch them am away
23:31   Still all things in this glade go thro
24:32   The stages of their quiet day.

         brick
45?:21   In the huge world that rumbles nigh
46?:22   Be others happy if they can;

*The numbers following the colon refer to line numbers of the final published version.
†This stanza was omitted from the final published version.

47?:23 But in my helpless cradle I
48?:24 Was looked on by the rural Pan

25:5 The birds sing sweetly in these trees
26:6 Across the girdling city's hum:
          among under the boughs
27:7 How green between the stems it is!
28:8 How strange the tremulous sheep-cries come

29:33 Then to their happy rest they pass.
30:34 The flowers close the birds are fed:
31:35 The night comes down upon the grass
          sweetly
32:36 The child sleeps warmly in his bed:

[Prose]   every day all these appear, live, go thro: their
stages whether I see them or no: I, in an unnatural
state of effort & personal wrappedupedness, do not see
them.
         Spirit who must be here
            —

33:37 Calm soul of all things .. make it mine
34:38 To feel amid the city's jar
35:39 That their° subsists a peace of thine
36:40 Man did not make & cannot mar
            —

37:41 The will to neither strive nor cry
38:42 The power to feel with others give:
39:43 Calm, calm me more. Nor let me die
40:44 Before I have begun to live.
            —

41:25 ~~But~~ I on men's impious tumult hurl'd
         sadly
42:26 Think sometimes as I hear them rave
43:27 That peace has left the upper world
44:28 And now dwells only in the grave.

[Spring 1849]

First known draft of "Lines written in Kensington Gardens."
A letter to his sister "K," dated simply "Thursday" but, like this
draft, written in 1849 (on the evidence of handwriting) and in
the spring (on internal evidence), includes a revised draft of the
poem. He mentions having written it "the other day lying in a
favorite glade of mine in Kensington gardens, & which I hope
may give you a feeling of the place & time."

The poem is one of a number written in 1849 not included
in the list headed "Comp.—1849" (25r–v, p. 114. Presumably,
it grew spontaneously out of the occasion.

Line 12: Cf. "in some unknown Power's employ" ("Stanzas
in Memory of the author of 'Obermann'" [1849], line 133).
Only during 1849–50 did A. use "employ" as a noun. Although
the aims of the two poems are different, many parallels exist.
"Kensington Gardens," from one point of view, is an exploration
of "the poet's" "two desires" in "Obermann," lines 93ff.

Lines 25–26: Cf. "Quiet Work" (lines 9–10).

Prose: In part, a summary of lines 22–24; the rest represents a lead that A. did not follow.

Line 33: The *anima mundi,* or world soul, of the Platonic
tradition and of Goethean and Wordsworthian nature poetry.
(See *P*, 272n and Honan, 94f.)

Line 34: Cf. "earthly jars" of "A Farewell," line 77.

Line 37: "neither strive nor cry" is from Matthew 12:19. Cf.
preface to *Essays in Criticism,* First Series (*CPW*, 3:286) and
"Stanzas from the Grande Chartreuse," line 120.

Lines 39–40: Cf. "So long as man knows not himself, he is
as if he existed not . . ." (Cousin, lecture 5 [1828], 35; trans.
Wight [1852], 1:86). Cf. Senancour, *Obermann,* letter 7, where
adjusting to existence means that you "will pass away forgetting
that you have never really lived" (Barnes, 1:43n; Michaut,
1:44n. In the same letter he attacks dilatoriness because "it
lets life slip away before one has reached the point at which
one really begins to live" (1:55; 1:54). Kenneth Allott (*P*,
273n) refers to a quotation from Rousseau in A.'s General
Notebook No. 1 (*N-Bs*, 463), but the handwriting indicates
that the entry was not made until about 1861.

Lines 41–42: Cf. "A Farewell," lines 85–88.

Lines 45–48?: Tinker and Lowry print this as the seventh stanza (*Commentary*, 197). A. probably composed it last and inserted it vertically in the right-hand margin of 11v, the only space available on either page. It was surely not intended either as the concluding stanza or as the seventh, where it interrupts the description of the glade and its life. It did not take its final position until 1867, having been omitted when the poem was first published in 1852.

[Feb., 1849/50]

See 34r [1–2], p. 212.

_____

[1] The object of the dramatic* poet being to represent others, no
     expression of the depth & high cultivation of his own being
     can be accepted in exchange of the performance of his object.
     Perhaps when young we sometimes represent best: for
     curiosity is then most active, & reflection least active: therefore
     we represent appearances in a lively natural & interested
     manner: whereas later our occupation with our own thoughts
     on man & society powerfully distracts us from the cheerful &
     unbiassed observing & recording of appearances. And if it is
     said that the mature & thoughtful poet abandons the outward
     appearances of objects to seize their inward being: I reply,
     that while the outward appearance & manners of men can be
     absolutely rendered; the requisites for such

_____

     rendering being lively curiosity & vigorous senses on the part
     of the poet: so the inward being of men, which is unseen, can
     never be absolutely rendered†: but the poet, endeavouring to
     put himself in the place of the person represented, tries his
     own soul in certain situations, and reports accordingly: a great
     opening being here left for the subjective & arbitrary.

[2] —Scott represents appearances: & for *dramatic effect* these are
     the indispensable. We can always supply an inward to an
     outward more readily than an outward to an inward.
     Shakspeare also represents appearances: hence his dramatic
     effect: he lends his own thoughts, however, to his characters,
     (within certain limits of manner & expression on their part:)
     hence his depth: but in *dramatic effect* he is perhaps, on this
     very account, inferior to Scott.

*"dramatic" added.
†"rendered" replaced "represented."

[Mar., 1849/50]

[1–2]   A.'s assertion of aesthetic principles is a product of his stock-taking, as well as an attempt to turn away from the writing of introspective poetry. It grew out of his work on "Empedocles" and plans for "Lucretius."

The major influence on these entries was Goethe, who raised the issues, even when A. goes his own way. In *Wilhelm Meisters Lehrjahre,* Goethe contrasts the characteristics of the drama with those of the novel or *Roman:* "In the 'Roman' should be set forth chiefly *States of mind* and *Events:* in the drama *Characters* and *Acts*" (A.'s translation of *Werke* [L.H.], 19:179–80; *Werke,* 7:330, un-published 1847 notebook).

Goethe (and Dr. Arnold) also thought very highly of Scott and praised his handling of appearances (*Werke,* 24:281, 473).

_____

He is a philosopher.

He has not the religious consolations of other men, facile because adapted to their weaknesses, or because shared by all around and charging the atmosphere they breathe. He sees things as they are—the world as it is—God as he is: in their stern simplicity.

The sight is a severe and mind-tasking one: to know the mysteries which are communicated to others by fragments, in parables.

But he started towards it in hope: his first glimpses of it filled him with joy: he had friends who shared his hope & joy & communicated to him theirs: even now he does not deny that the sight is capable of affording rapture & the purest peace.

But his friends are dead: the world is all against him, & incredulous of the truth: his mind is overtasked by the effort to hold fast so great & severe

_____

a truth in solitude: the atmosphere he breathes not being modified by the presence of human life, is too rare for him. He perceives still the truth of the truth, but cannot be transported and rapturously agitated by his* grandeur: his spring and elasticity of mind are gone: he is clouded, oppressed, dispirited, without hope & energy.

Before he becomes the victim of depression & overtension of mind, to the utter deadness to joy, grandeur, spirit, and animated life, he desires to die; to be reunited with the universe, before by exaggerating his human side he has become utterly estranged from it.

_____

*"its" is meant.

[Mar., 1849/50]

This is neither a complete outline for "Empedocles on Etna" nor a scenario or a biographical sketch, but a synopsis of Empedocles' reasons for living and for dying. It presents the central issues of the poem only insofar as they are embodied in the outlook and state of mind of Empedocles and in the crisis that leads to his suicide.

This entry indicates that within a year of choosing the topic A. had worked out the central features of Empedocles' dilemma. None of it depends upon A.'s research. This summary makes plain that A. wanted to create a *modern* culture hero, such as Faust, Manfred, or Obermann—all of whom share something with their authors.

Rough drafts of stanzas for "Empedocles," I.ii, survive under the heading "Lucretius" (*Commentary*, 293–94), indicating that A. appropriated materials originally written for that work. The comments here provide, in addition, a sketch for many of Empedocles' reflections in act II. But with the possible exception of "The Pillars of the Universe" no drafts or notes have survived touching on Callicles' lyrics or on Pausanias' speeches. It is likely that they were not conceived until at least 1850, when the increasing length of the poem made clear that more than a lyric structure would be necessary.

A.'s analysis of Empedocles in part grows out of his concern at this time with "spiritual distress," "intellectual & spiritual Vision," and Froude's view of the needs of "the Spiritual" that cannot be met by social or political action. See 33r[2–3], 17r, pp. 139, 142.

"The truth" is Empedocles' vision of the oneness of all things: "the world as it is—God as he is: in their stern simplicity." (Cf. 9r[3], p. 186.)

——————————————————————

[3]   —no remodelling of society can make the world delightful to
      the Spiritual: but it *can* make it agreeable, comparatively, to
      the herd. (Froude)

      ——————

[1]   We learn not to *abuse* or *storm at* the Gods or Fate: knowing
      this mere madness: as there is nothing wilfully operating
      against us—the only object of anger: and the power we would
      curse is the same with ourselves: the same with the tongue
      employed to articulate the curse. God patiently lends himself
      to curse himself.—

      ——————

[2]   —The poet, says Caesar, laughs at men for giving an absolute
      value to wealth or power: but does not he pursue an absolute
      happiness, a euhemeric, a bien être, that of intellectual or
      spiritual Vision?

——————————————————————

[Mar., 1849/50]

Everything on this page deals with the nature of happiness, the means
of achieving it, or man's anger at failing to achieve it.

[1]   This entry forms the basis for much of "Empedocles on Etna,"
I.ii.272–305. Cf. a rejected stanza intended for the same speech,
26r, stanza 1, and 23r, pp. 209 and 192, for a view of God
compatible with this comment.
         In the published poem, A. omitted from Empedocles' advice
to Pausanias any reference to the phrase "knowing this mere
madness," probably because Empedocles has his own form of
madness. About 1850, the cluster of ideas involved in the concept of madness was very important to A. See pp. 16–18.

[2]   A. invented this speech. It was probably intended for "Lucretius," which he continued to work on even while writing
"Empedocles." Julius Caesar was the classical political figure who
most interested A. (see commentary on 34r, pp. 213ff.). Dr.
Arnold had written at length on him (*Encyclopaedia Metropolitana*,
10) and always insisted that the classics be read in the light of
their total cultural relevance, a tradition A. carried on.
         "euhemeric": a coinage based on the Greek εὐημερία (health
and wealth, happiness). (Cf. "Eutrapelia" in "A Speech at Eton,"
thirty years later, *CPW*, 9:23–26 and passim.)

[3]   Despite the fact that the passage attributed to Froude is at
the top of the page, it is squeezed in and obviously was written
last. It also has closer ties to entry 2 than to 1.
         James Anthony Froude (1818–94), historian, biographer and
critic, attended Oriel College, Oxford, and became a fellow of
Exeter College. As an admirer of Dr. Arnold and a close friend
of Clough, he naturally got to know A., who, in turn, was particularly interested in Froude's reactions to his poetry. (See *CL*,
127n, and Dunn, *Froude*, 1:134.) In a letter of October 31,
1853, to "K," A. remarked, "You—Froude—Shairp—I believe
the list of those whose reading of me I anticipate with pleasure
stops there or thereabouts" (*UL*, 20–21; the short list kept

varying). A.'s first volume of poems and Froude's novel of religious doubt, *The Nemesis of Faith,* were published almost simultaneously at the end of February, 1849. Froude finally resigned his fellowship, having been *"preached* against" in Chapel and having had his book *"burnt* publicly" at his college (Dunn, 1:135).

Since Froude's comment does not seem to have been taken from any of his published work, it probably comes from a letter or from conversation. It corresponds with views expressed in print as early as his Chancellor Prize Essay, "The Influence of the Science of Political Economy on the Moral and Social Welfare of a Nation" (1842).

In a letter of January° 7, 1852, A. translates Froude into his own terms:

> I am more and more convinced that the world tends to become more comfortable for the mass, and more uncomfortable for those of any natural gift or distinction—and it is as well perhaps that it should be so. . . . [T]he world might do worse than to dismiss too high pretentions, and settle down on what it can see and handle and appreciate." (*CL,* 122–23)

Cf. A.'s comments on "spiritual distress" (17r, p. 142); his discussion of the need for moral and intellectual deliverance (*CPW,* 1:19); and the contrast between Empedocles and Pausanias in "Empedocles on Etna."

Entries 2 and 3 point toward *Culture and Anarchy,* especially *CPW,* 5:94–95 and 106–7.

A man may fall into spiritual distress at 2 periods of the
world. Either at a period when the belief in a God is
(generally) universal—

        or

when, tho: prevalent among the vulgar, this belief is amongst
thinkers losing ground.

————————

at the first period the issue from spiritual distress will be
probably to fervent religion:
—at the second to a mastery over oneself & the world.
—Confusion* arises from taking the step

out of harmony with the period.
    Bruno — Maurice.
in England where the movement of the world is not known or
observed the wrong step may be repeatedly taken.

*"Confusion" replaced "Misery."

[Mar., 1849/50]

The principal source of A.'s knowledge of Bruno (1548–1600) was Emile Saisset, "Giordano Bruno et la philosophie au seizième siècle," *RDM,* June 15, 1847, 1071–1105, a review article occasioned by the publication of Christian Bartholmess's two-volume study *Jordano Bruno.* To A., in the midst of writing "Empedocles on Etna," this religious philosopher, scientist, poet, playwright, and doubter must have seemed another avatar. He prepared the way for modern science, but he viewed himself confusedly as attempting to return to the purity of the past. Agitated by an infinite *inquiétude* (another of A.'s restless wanderers), he doubted, yet needed to believe. But instead of finding fulfillment in returning to fervent religion, his independence led him to the stake.

(John) Frederick Denison Maurice (1805–72), the son of a Unitarian minister, experienced a conversion to orthodox trinitarian Christianity in his mid-twenties, was baptized in the Church of England in 1831 and ordained three years later. Soon he was defending the universities' use of the Thirty-nine Articles that had earlier prevented him from obtaining a law degree at Cambridge. By 1846, he had become chaplain to Lincoln's Inn and professor of theology at King's College, London. After the failure of the Chartist petition of 1848, Maurice became one of the leaders of the new Christian Socialist Movement.

Maurice had moved from unbelief to fervent faith; yet his intellect and conscience would not permit him to accept the theological dogmas of any religious party (*Life of Maurice,* 2:11). For A.'s reaction to Maurice, see *L,* January 7, 1863 (to his mother); *CPW,* 6:383; 10:226–27.

A.'s comments emphasize Maurice's confusion, which he attributes to England's ignorance of the world. In an unpublished letter to his sister "K," A. observed: "England has fallen intellectually so far behind the Continent[,] . . . we may expect to see English people doing things which have long been done & see discovering what has been discovered and used up elsewhere . . ." (May 11, [1850], in Balliol College Library, Oxford; cf. *L,* May, 1848, to the same).

This entry anticipates by nearly two decades A.'s line of reasoning in the concluding paragraph of "Hebraism and Hellenism" (*CPW*, 5:175).

[1a] The misery of the present age is not in the intensity of men's
      suffering—but in their incapacity to suffer, enjoy, feel at all,
      wholly & profoundly—in their having their susceptibility
      eternally agacée by a continual dance of ever-changing objects,
      and not having the power to attach it upon one, to expend it
[1b] on that one, to absorb it in that one: in their being ever
      learning & never coming to the knowledge of the truth: in
      their having a presentiment of all things, a possession of none:
      in their having one moment the commencement of a feeling,
      at the next* moment the commencement of an imagination, at
      the next the commencement of a thought & the eternal
      tumult of the world mingling, breaking in upon, hurrying
[1c] away all. Deep suffering is the consciousness of oneself no less
      than deep enjoyment. The disease of the present age is
      divorce from oneself.

*"the next" replaced "another."

[June, 1849/50]

A. wrote this important entry on the first page of the notebook portion of the *YMS*. He progresses from "misery" to "disease" in his analysis of what he elsewhere calls these "damned times" (*CL*, 111; Sept. 23, 1849). He anatomizes them here not in terms of institutions or beliefs but in terms of the individual man's private experience. Cf. Carlyle, "Characteristics" (*Works*, 28:1–43).

[1a]   Men have "never deeply felt, nor clearly will'd" ("The Scholar-Gipsy," 173; see *P*, 365n). Iris Sells calls attention to Charles de Rémusat's description ([1847], 1:120°) of some of A.'s favorite romantic protagonists—Werther, René, and Ortis—as "tormented at once by the need and the powerlessness to feel and believe" (Sells, *Matthew Arnold and France*, 102).
     "agacée": irritated.
     See "The Scholar-Gipsy," lines 142–46, 167, 204; "Tristram and Iseult," III.119, 123–24; "Memorial Verses," line 46. The result described here is a special form of "wandering," which A. usually calls "restlessness" ("Stanzas from the Grande Chartreuse," line 104, the counterpart of the "eternally restless mind" of "Empedocles on Etna," II.330; cf. "A Farewell," lines 27–28). The Breton bard of "Tristram and Iseult" sees "diseased unrest" as the result of any obsession (III.135). See also "A Summer Night," lines 27–33. Cf. Goethe, *Dichtung und Wahrheit* (*Werke*, 10:508). For the difficulty A. found in following this advice, see 11r[1], p. 180.
     In a letter of "the late spring or summer of 1850" to Wyndham Slade, he tells of his disappointment when "for the 5th time the deities interposed" and prevented him from seeing a certain "young lady" (Miss Wightman). He concludes by using the same French participle: "all the oppositiveness & wilfulness in the human breast is agacée by a succession of these perverse disappointments" (*Commentary*, 170).

[1b]   For the fragmentary and aimless nature of human experience, see "Empedocles on Etna," I.ii.84–85; "The Scholar-Gipsy," lines 165, 168–69, 176–77; "The Lord's Messengers," lines 13–14. The letters to Clough are full of complaints about

distractions that lead to fluctuating and about the need for self-mastery (*CL*, 110–11, 130, 138, 146). Later prose works reflect a similar vision (*CPW*, 3:30–32; 6:179). A.'s reflections anticipate much of Walter Pater's "Conclusion" (1868) to *The Renaissance* (*Works*, 1:233–39), even though their goals for man are diametrically opposed.

[1c]   Because man is divorced from himself, he is incapable of deep suffering as well as deep enjoyment. A. returns to where he began these reflections, but now he supplies the cause of the disease—alienation from self. See "Self-Dependence," lines 1–2; "Empedocles on Etna," I.ii.128–31, 142–43.

This entry points toward one of the central themes of A.'s preface to *Poems* (1853): tragic suffering can give rise to poetic enjoyment; but merely morbid and painful situations, "in which there is everything to be endured, nothing to be done," cannot produce aesthetic pleasure (*CPW*, 1:2–3).

Almost certainly the first draft of "Tristram and Iseult,"
III.1-2, 5-37.

1, 5   The year had travell'd round, & one bright day

6   Drew Iseult forth—her children were at play

            a

7   In that green circular opening in the heath

8   Which borders the sea shore—a country path

                  fields

9 Steals   Creeps over it from the till'd land behind—

                     are

10   The openings° grassy banks were soft inclined

   Yet low—& from the bottom Yet to one standing in it

11   But their slope was not deep—and far & near

               goes spreading

12   The lone unbroken view stretch'd bright & clear

              All th°   hollow

{ 13   Over the waste: but where the open ground

                  This ring

       leaves   encircling

{ 14   First meets the fringing heath at once all round

     Is green & clear—the heather which all round

    Is light & green

{ 15   The heather disappears, and the pale grass

  Creeps Blooms thickly, grows not here

16   Is strewn with rocks & many a shiverd mass

17   Of vein'd white gleaming quartz, & here & there

18   Sprinkld with holly trees & juniper

            In the smooth centre

19   Down in the middle of the hollow stood

22   With scarlet berries bright the fellfare's food

20   Three hollies side by side, & made a screen

21   Where the sun's rays fla struck full, & flash'd back keen.

23   Under the burnish'd hollies Iseult stands

24   Watching her children play: their little hands

25   Are busy gathe[r]ing spars of quartz, and streams

26   Of stagshorn for their hats: anon, with screams

27   Of mad delight they drop their spoils & bou[n]d

28   Amo[n]g the holly clumps & broken grou[n]d

29   Racing full speed, & startling in their rush

30   The fellfares & the speckld mistle thrush

31   Out of their glossy coverts: but when now
32   Their cheeks grew* flush'd, & over each hot brow
33   Under the featherd hats of the sweet pair
34   In blinding masses shower'd the golden hair—
35   Then Iseult call'd them to her and the three
36   Clusterd under the holly screen, & she
37   Told them an old world Breton history

1   A year had flown and in the chapel old
2   Lay Tristran & queen Iseult dead & cold

*Written over "were."

[Sept., 1849/June, 1850]

This is almost certainly the first draft of "Tristram and Iseult," III.1–2, 5–37.[1] The lines are numbered here to correspond with the final version. Lines 34–37 and 1–2 have been written in the left-hand margin at right angles to lines 5–33. The handwriting does not suggest that the lines in the margin were written appreciably later. In fact, the placement of the revisions "Is light & green" (line 14) and "Creeps" (15) reveals that they were written after the lines in the margin. The following list details the substantive revisions in the published versions. (A.'s numerous changes in spelling and punctuation have not been noted, because they were of only minor concern to him in first drafts.) Unless otherwise noted, A. retained the revisions made in this draft.

Line 5: "The year had travell'd round, &" became "The young surviving Iseult,"; although originally intended as the first line of this section, it makes no mention of Tristram or Iseult of Ireland.

Line 6: "Drew Iseult" became "Had wander'd."

Line 7: "opening" became "hollow."

Line 9: A. returned to his original choice, "Creeps." He probably substituted "Steals" when he changed "Blooms" to "Creeps" (line 15) but then decided it was too imprecise.

Line 10: "openings" became "hollow's."

Line 11: 1852ff., became "And to one standing on them, far and near." The physical standpoint seems to have given A. some trouble. He changed "from the bottom" to his final version when he decided that an elevated position was obviously preferable for viewing the surrounding landscape.

Line 12: "goes spreading" became "spreads." The revision avoids introducing an unnecessary hexameter line.

Line 13: "but where the open ground" in 1852 became "This ring of open ground"; in 1853, "This cirque of open ground." A. revised this line so much that the presence of "This ring" in the manuscript has gone undetected.

Line 14: A.'s manuscript revision eliminates "clear" to avoid repeating the rhyme word in line 12.

Line 15: 1852ff., became "Creeps thickly, grows not here;

but the pale grass." A.'s internal manuscript revisions make the line more precise.

Line 18: "Sprinkld" became "Dotted."

Line 19: "hollow" became "opening"; A. vacillated between these two words (lines 7, 10, 13). The idea of a hollow seems to have occurred to him first in line 13. He then decided to emphasize Iseult's refuge as a hollow (7 and 10) and only later and secondarily as an opening (13 and 19). The idea of a hollow, along with the screen of holly trees, is essential to create the image of a protected spot. Describing it as an opening helps to set it apart from its surroundings. Together they help create a shelter that has much in common with the forest glade of the Breton tale of Merlin and Vivian and many another glade in A.'s poetry.

Lines 20–22: A. rearranged the order of these lines for the sake of syntactical clarity. The new arrangement meant splitting a couplet, a startling departure from the pattern he had established.

Line 22; "bright" became "gemm'd"; this revision avoids repeating "bright," used in lines 5 and 12. It also helps to create a rather dazzling sunny scene, even if there is only a winter sun. It contrasts with A's more common moonlit scenes.

Line 21: 1852ff., became "Warm with the winter-sun, of burnish'd green." The revision eliminates the weak final phrase and the slow heavy movement of the line, especially the second and third feet. It is still not wholly satisfactory.

Line 23: "burnish'd" became "glittering"; reinforces the revision of line 22 and is necessitated by the shift of "burnish'd" to line 21.

Line 32: "grew" became "were"; A. reverted to his original choice as the more accurate.

Lines 1–2: The same as the published version of 1852, except that A. uses the spelling "Tristran" here, halfway between the "Tristan" of his French source and his final "Tristram." These were the last lines to be written on this page and are a partial substitute for the first line on this page.

When A. became aware through Dunlop's *History of Fiction* (87) that Tristram and Iseult had been buried in Cornwall, he revised lines 1 and 2 and added two new lines:

A year had flown, and o'er the sea away
In Cornwall, Tristram and Queen Iseult lay;
At Tyntagil, in King Marc's chapel old:
There in a ship they bore those lovers cold.

Finally, in 1857, he revised line 3 in order to reflect the correct pronunciation of Tyntágel: "In King Marc's chapel, in Tyntagel old—."

Of the first fifteen lines, only line 8 remains as A. first wrote it. The most popular part of this section, that dealing with the children (who were A.'s invention) required no substantial revision. The complex symbolism of the landscape, especially lines 9–15, caused him much difficulty. The problem was to keep his eye on the object and still convey the appropriate metaphorical implications.

NOTE ON DATING

1. In a letter to Herbert Hill, his former private tutor, A. wrote: "I read the story of Tristram and Iseult some years ago at Thun . . ." (Nov. 5, 1852; *TLS*, May 19, 1932, 368). A. gave the same account years later to Horace Maule in a letter of August 17, 1870 (Davis, *Arnold's Letters*, facing 211). The handwriting supports the generally accepted view that A. is referring to his second trip to Thun in September, 1849, rather than the one a year earlier when a tale of doomed and ravaging love would not have seemed so compelling a subject.

[1a] Goethe on writing destroying thought—yes—and expression
also—'tis that the two modes are incompatable°—a total
change takes place in the man in passing from one to the
other

[1b] to reflect—to turn the attention back upon a past phenomenon
or series of phenomena, instead of letting it travel forwards
over the eternally rising new phenomena of the moment.
Not to mirror. But this operation loses the contents
of the moment.

[2] —The yearning of Christ to the multitude—the solitariness of
the philosopher: the longing of the man who has gained the
shore towards the infinite Ocean behind him: the desire for
the all which makes content impossible

[3] —a man may write a book thro: whose head all manner of
fruitful thoughts have passed: & yet the daemon shall not
allow him to put more than one of them into it. Guizot's why
has the G. R. réussi? 62.

[July, 1849/50]

[1]   This is not a paraphrase but apparently a conclusion reached
after reading widely in Goethe's works. Entry 1b provides A.'s
explanation for 1a. Among the passages that may lie behind
this observation are: "Schlussbetrachtung über Sprache und
Terminologie," *Zur Farbenlehre,* sections 751 and 754 (*Werke,*
16:203–4); a lyric from "Urtheilsworte französischer Kri-
tiker" (*Werke,* 14:781); letter to Schiller, February 19, 1802
(*Werke,* 20:881).
        Cf. "Empedocles on Etna," I.ii.82–86, and "Lucretius," frag-
ment ii (*P,* 648). See also 13r[4] and 6r[2], pp. 70 and 171.

[2]   The inescapable separation of the writer from the doer and
even from himself leads to this brief list of aliens. A. wrote many
poems that touch upon the peculiar isolation of the poet or
thinker as well as others that involve the general theme of alienation. In connection with the Faustian "desire for the all," note
A.'s listing prominently among the poems to be composed in
1849 two involving "refusal of limitation" (25r, p. 114). Cf.
4r[4], p. 195.

[Feb., 1852/53]

[3]   This entry points to another form of limitation. A. is probably
thinking of Goethe's frequent references to the daemonic, a power
neither human nor divine, beyond our rational control. (See
letter to his mother, in *L,* Mar. 3, 1865). Cf. pp. 23–24,
6r[2], p. 171.
        "G. R.": the Glorious Revolution.
        The reference is to page 62 of the first edition of François
Guizot, *Pourquoi la révolution d'Angleterre a-t-elle réussi? Discours sur
l'histoire de la révolution d'Angleterre* (1850), a pamphlet intended
to introduce a new edition of his *Histoire de la révolution d'Angleterre*
(1826–27), which Dr. Arnold included in the French curric-
ulum for the sixth form at Rugby. For A.'s extensive use of this
pamphlet see the commentary for 34r (pp. 213–14).
        The conservative Guizot was the most important minister in

Louis-Philippe's regime. When it was overthrown in 1848, Guizot fled to England for a year. A. first met Guizot in 1859 and gives him high praise throughout his investigation of *The Popular Education of France* (1861).

A. probably read Sainte-Beuve's review of Guizot's discourse, collected in volume 1 of *Causeries de lundi* (1851), which he took with him on his honeymoon.

38 Warm in their mantles wrapt, the three stay'd there
Under the hollies in the clear still air—
Mantles with those deep furs rich glistering
Which Venice ships do from swarth Egypt bring.
Long they stay'd still then, pacing at their eyes°
43 Mov'd up & down under their glossy trees
But still as they pusud* their warm dry road
From Iseult's lips the unbroken story flow'd
And still the children listend their blue eyes
Fix'd on their mother's face in wide surprize—
48 Nor did their looks stray once to the seaside
Nor to the brown heaths round them warm & wide—
Nor to the snow which though 'twas all away
From th'open waste, white by the hedgerows lay—
Nor to the shining seafowl that with screams
53 Came in from where the bright Atlantic gleams
Swooping to landward nor to where, quite clear
The fell-fares settld on the thickets near;
And they would still have listend till dark night
Came keen & chill† down on the heather bright,
58 But when the red glow on the sea grew cold
And the grey turrets of the castle old
Look'd ste[r]nly thro: the frosty eve[n]ing air
Then Iseult took by the ha[n]d those children fair
And brought her tale to an end, & fou[n]d the path
63 And led them home over the darke[n]ing heath.

---

*"pursu'd" intended.
†Written over d.

[Sept., 1849/July 1850]

A few days, perhaps—certainly not more than a few weeks—elapsed between the composition of the opening lines of part III of "Tristram and Iseult" (2v) and this continuation. A. now spells "fell-fares" (line 55) as he does in his final version, rather than "fellfare" (lines 22, 30).

It is difficult to understand why A. skipped from sheet 2v to 1ov when he resumed writing part III. If 3r was already partially filled by the time he was ready to go on with the poem, he may have decided to put it on the first blank two-page spread, working from the back of the notebook, which was then entirely given over to poetry. (No rearranging of the order of the sheets can eliminate the difficulty.) A. regularly skipped back and forth in the notebook, but no other poem is divided in this way.

The fact that these lines contain no revisions seems to suggest that this is not a first draft, although the first draft of lines 23–37 (2v, pp. 149–50) contains only one revision.

His careless writing of "eyes," when he meant "ease" (line 42), and his beginning to write "down" before "chill" (57) suggest that he had already composed at least this part of the poem in his head. "Eyes" are extremely important, so this kind of slip is not surprising. At times his mind raced ahead of his pencil.

A. changed the following words when he published the poem in 1852. The final version retained all of the revisions.

Line 38: "stay'd" became "stood." "[S]tay'd" may have suggested greater permanence than A. wanted to suggest. "[S]tood" helps to create a sharper visual image.

Line 40: "deep furs rich" became "rich furs deep"; more precise.

Line 41: "swarth" became "swart"; for the sake of the sound.

Line 42: "eyes" became "ease"; a slip of the pencil.

Line 43: "their" became "the"; "Their" in 44 is enough.

Line 49: "warm" became "bright"; this harks back to the opening lines. A. found it advisable to use "warm" less frequently in the first section, but by line 49 he had not used the word for twenty-seven lines (thirty-seven lines in the final version). The revision also eliminates any possible confusion between snow and warm heaths.

Line 51: "waste, white" became "heath, still"; A. opts for "heath[s]" in this section (cf. lines 49, 63). In the opening section he uses "waste" as well.

Line 53: "Came in" became "Bore up"; more vigorous and avoids beginning two lines with the same verb (line 57).

A. altered only the punctuation in the remaining ten lines.

Line 44: "road" is not the "path" that leads home but simply their way within the hollow that they pursue in their pacing (line 42). Yet, somehow, despite this movement, their eyes remain "Fix'd on their mother's face" (line 47).

Line 45: Iseult is a passive vehicle for the story she tells. It comes from her lips but not from her experience.

Line 47: Their "wide[-eyed] surprize" echoes "the wild surmise" of Cortez's men in Keats's sonnet "On First Looking into Chapman's Homer."

[1]   The Roman world perished for having disobeyed reason and nature.

     The infancy of the world was renewed with all its sweet illusions

     but infancy and its illusions must for ever be transitory, and we are again in the place of the Roman world, our illusions past, debtors to the service of reason & nature.

     O let us beware how we again are false to them: we shall perish, and the world will be renewed: but we shall leave the same question to be solved by a future age.

[2]   —I cannot conceal from myself the objection which really wounds & perplexes me from the religious side is that the service of reason is freezing to feeling, chilling to the religious mood*.

     & feeling & the religious mood are eternally the deepest being of man, the ground of all joy & greatness for him.

*"the religious mood" replaced "religious moods."

[Aug., 1849/50]

[1]   A. shared his father's belief that the Roman world of Caesar
and Cicero was the greatest of all modern societies, despite the
fact that it had failed to produce an adequate literature.

    "Reason" means right reason, the voice of God, conscience,
natural law, or man's "best self." It leads man to seek out and
follow the universal or providential order that seems aimed at
in the world.

    Illusions are "sweet" because they are associated with child-
hood, but they are appropriate only to the infancy of a culture.

    Some twenty-five years later, A. returned to this entry for the
line "The infancy of the world was renewed, with all its sweet
illusions" (preface to *God and the Bible*, *CPW*, 7:386). But he
completely altered its implications. In 1875, A. was less concerned with the loss of Roman civilization ("civilisation could
build itself up again") than with the "indispensable" contribution
of Christianity. Without the overthrow of Rome, Christianity
could not have established itself in the form it did. With all its
miraculous elements, it required a credulous world. This points
toward the next entry.

[2]   Having put the case for reason, A. now looks at its negative
side, from the point of view of religion. Reason now loses its
moral connotations and comes close to being simply analytical
and abstract thought.

    A. may have recalled two comments by Goethe: "Men con-
tinue to be creative in poetry and art only so long as they are
religious . . ." (*Conversations with Riemer*, July, 1810, Weigand,
45; *Werke*, 22:597) and "The only religion that can be of use
must be simple and warm" ("Two Important as Yet Undiscussed
Biblical Questions," Weigand, 45; *Werke*, 4:140). Kenneth
Allott finds a parallel in Sainte-Beuve's 1844 essay on Leo-
pardi, reprinted in *Portraits contemporains* (1884), 4:411 (quoted
in *E & S*, n.s., 21 [1968]: 95–96). It expresses the same general attitude as this entry but without the imagery of chill (or
warmth). (Cf. *CL*, 143.)

    A. touches on the tensions between philosophy and religion,

thought and feeling, cold and warmth in "Stanzas in Memory of the Author of 'Obermann,' " lines 87–88, 107, "Stanzas from the Grande Chartreuse," lines 67–69 (1855 version), and "Progress," lines 16–19, 25–28 (1852 version). A.'s search for a way of synthesizing these oppositions led years later to his concept of the "imaginative reason."

With "Obermann Once More" (Oct., 1865–Mar., 1867), A. tried to revive his creative impulses by returning not only to the earlier poem on Obermann but also to this manuscript, drawing upon both its entries. The two Obermann poems, however, are poles apart in outlook. While the sequel touches on all the facts of these entries, it transforms them, giving A.'s early perplexity an optimistic resolution and ignoring the warning, "O let us beware how we again are false to [reason and nature]."

[1]   We have a will
        we find we cannot freely give it scope
        we are irritated, & account for it on different theories into
    which we carry our irritation.
        but look at the matter calmly
    We arrive, a new force in a schon existent world of forces.
        our force can only have play so far as these other forces will
    let it.
        the confusion & sinfulness of men wᶜ͟h *we* are avoiding will
    continue to throw obstacles in our way even when we are cured
    ourselves of it.
                    ——————

[2]   You find what answers to the yearning of your inmost soul
        therein do you: my god, let us tell him that, for he cannot
        find what answers to that of his own in it
                    ——————

[3]   we will not dwell on our own past because we cannot think it
        worth dwelling on & arranging, & hope for something better
        in the future.—*

*See 5r[4] (p. 165) for entry completed at the bottom of this page.

[Aug., 1849/50]

[1]   A. could have found similar comments in Eckermann's *Gespräche mit Goethe* for December 6, 1829, and in Goethe's verses on "Necessity," from his "Primal Orphic Sayings" (*Werke*, 1:523).

This entry provided the basis for several parts of Empedocles' address to Pausanias in "Empedocles on Etna," I.ii, especially lines 182–86 and 242–46. Instead of "refusal of limitation" 25r[4], p. 114, there is the Stoic necessity of coming to terms with limitation, as in "The Sick King in Bokhara," "Resignation," "[To a Republican Friend] Continued," lines 5–8, and "Courage," lines 1–4. Cf. 5v[2], p. 168.

[2]   Interpretation depends upon the referent of "therein" and the tone of the speaker.

Cf. "In Utrumque Paratus," 40.

A.'s poems about the "inmost soul" usually show man alienated from the world around him, from himself, or from both.

[3]   This and entry 2 may have been intended for a quasi-dramatic poem.

Cf. Senancour, *Obermann*, letter 90 (Michaut, 2:236).

[1]   Je ne me suis pas refugié avec un Dieu humain, exclusif, anti
      naturel—no, I take myself to witness &c

[2]   —We have been on a thousand lines & on each have shown
      spirit talent even geniality but hardly for an hour between
      birth & death have we been on our own one natural line, have
      we been ourselves, have we breathed freely.

[3]   —To feel simply the simple feelings of humanity voilà the
      natural life of man: to prolong fix & dwell upon these by
      harmoniously expressing them, voilà the natural life of the
      poet. And art—what can be done more than to arrange in the
      best way so as to produce the fullest most undisturbed effect—
      to recount a fact of interest with the most perfect limpidity.
      The more perfectly the poet can throw himself into the
      circumstances he deals with the more perfectly he will feel the
      greater or less truth of his relation or version of them. Life is
      before the narration of life. Narrative
                Is but the pal'd & waning shadow of fact

[4]   —His observation of the circumstance under wch he has

      rendered his version most limpid may suggest much to him in
      the way of rules: but the form generally should change with
      each new matter. But a cramp'd pis-aller life has produced a
      cramp'd pis-aller poetry.

[Aug., 1849/50]

[1] "I have not taken refuge in a human, exclusive God, opposed to nature—"

"[A]nti naturel" is an Arnoldian coinage. The entire entry may represent his phrasing.

The entry relates to the topic: "Empedocles—refusal of limitation by the religious sentiment" (25r[4], p. 114). A. made use of this note in "Empedocles on Etna," II.399–403. Empedocles' attempt to put himself in tune with the order of nature is primarily Stoic.

The entry helps to make clear that many of these notes do not express A.'s individual views but are intended to be put into the mouth of a character or are expressions representing the outlook of any sensitive, intelligent person.

[2] The idea that every man has "one natural line" underlies A.'s disdain for most men who, like himself, "fluctuate idly" ("The Scholar-Gipsy," lines 167–69). Cf. CL, 110. "A Speech at Eton" (1879; CPW, 9:35) reveals how much A.'s views on this topic changed over the years.

"[B]reathed freely" suggests the stoic idea that freedom is not a matter of doing as one pleases but of finding out what is appropriate, what one ought to do and then doing it. (Cf. 4v[1], p. 163.) A. frequently associates this kind of freedom with having an abundance of air, breathing without constraint. (See "Youth's Agitations," line 6; "Revolutions," line 20; "A Summer Night," line 90; and "Empedocles on Etna," II.408, to list only the most striking examples. Cf. 13r[2], p. 70.) According to Senancour, only among solitary mountains or in similar regions "man recovers [his] true self . . . he breathes a free air untainted by the exhalations of social life. . . . [H]e lives a real life of his own in the sublime unity of things" (Obermann, letter 7; Barnes, 1:42–43; Michaut, 1:43–44).

A. developed the idea in The Popular Education of France (1861): "Life itself consists, say the philosophers, in the effort to affirm one's own essence; meaning by this, to develop one's own existence fully and freely, to have ample light and air, to be neither cramped nor overshadowed" (CPW, 2:7).

[3]   Affective and mimetic theories of poetry are juxtaposed but not synthesized here. See the Introduction (pp. 25–29) for a discussion of A.'s poetics.

His emphasis upon the relationship between literature and life probably owes something to Goethe. In a letter to his mother of May 7, 1849°, A. praises Goethe's "thorough sincerity—writing about nothing that he had not experienced" (*L*). In "Noch ein Wort für junge Dichter," Goethe urges young poets: "do but ask yourselves at every Poem—if it contains an actual experience . . ." (A.'s trans., from his unpublished 1847 notebook; *Werke* [L.H.], 45; *Werke*, 14:399; see also Eckermann, *Gespräche mit Goethe*, Sept. 18, 1823, and March 14, 1830.)

[4]   The emphasis here is Aristotelian or inductive, but with a marked Coleridgean flavor—form follows function or matter, so that, because the matter always varies, the form of each work is essentially unique.

The final sentence is a corollary of "life before the narration of life." In A.'s *The Popular Education of France* (1861), a cramped life is the antithesis of one in which man can breathe freely and affirm his own essence (see entry 2 above).

This is a strange sentence. The use of the apostrophe in "cramp'd" is characteristic of A.'s poetry, not his prose, and the shift in tense to "*has* produced," when one expects either the present or future tense, suggests not a general comment on the connection between poetry and life but a comment on the work of a specific poet. (The sentence itself is cramped—squeezed in at the bottom of the page opposite the one on which he began it.) Possibly, A. intended to draw on this, too, for a poem. He uses the noun *pis-aller*—a last resort, a makeshift, what one accepts when one can do no better—as an adjective. This is a life-for-art's-sake position. (A's late poem "Pis-aller" owes nothing to this entry.)

All these entries confront the problem of being "natural" as a man and as an artist—that is, being attuned to the universal order or the will of the only kind of god A. then believed in. (See 9r[4] and 23r, pp. 186 and 192.)

[1]   The truth we saw intuitively we deal with mechanically—the
      work we conceived vitally we too often execute deadly. triste
      race humaine.

[2]   Nature has long since kept this inn, the Earth, & seen
      so many successive floods of guests with their fashions &
      ridiculousnesses that no swagger of any new comer can
      impose upon her.

[3]   —nothing makes me more despise the world than the homage
      it pays to experience. To mock at feeling, to live recklessly, to
      enter a mauvais lieu at your ease—all this, the world seems to
      think, implies a possessing of the scrupulous mind full of its
      delicacies and apprehensions* & newnesses, & at the same
      time of the philosophy wͨh overcomes this: but it generally
      implies only the total absence of all youth & richness of soul,
      and the presence of a dead barren negative callosity—not
      pleasant to the possessor.

[4]   —The feeling with wͨh a man of the world reads in books of
      sentiment & its graduall° Suffocation in the world, after he
      himself has had his suffocated.

*"apprehensions" replaced "waywardnesses."

[Aug., 1849/50]

[1]   "triste race humaine": sad human race (cf. 8r[2], p. 203),
unhappy mankind.
    A. may be recalling Goethe's comments in "Schlussbetrach-
tung über Sprache und Terminologie" (Concluding Observations on Terminology) from *Zur Farbenlehre*, section 754: "how
difficult it is to avoid substituting the sign for the thing; how
difficult to keep the essential quality still living before us, and
not to kill it with the word" (trans. Eastlake [1820] in *Goethe's
Color Theory*, 257; *Werke*, 16:204; cf. 3r[1] and 9r[5], pp.
154 and 186). The context suggests that A. was thinking of
the difficulty not only of sincere verbal communication but also
of living according to one's convictions in relationships with
others. Cf. "Switzerland."

[2]   A shortened version of this comment, two lines of blank verse,
became the epigraph of "The Future" (1853, 1854):

        For Nature hath long kept this inn, the Earth,
        And many a guest hath she therein receiv'd—

This motto omits, because irrelevant to the poem, the idea that
man must adjust to Nature and not expect her to change her
ways for him. A. made use of that idea in "Empedocles on Etna,"
I.ii.217–21; cf. 207–8. The more general image of man as a
stranger or traveler is reflected in "Empedocles on Etna," I.ii.181
and II.350, and in "Lucretius," fragment vi (*P*, 650). Cf. 4v[1],
p. 163.

[3]   "mauvais lieu": bad place, difficult situation.
    This entry suggests, as does entry 1, that A.'s feelings were
undergoing a severe testing. Even more than entry 1, this comment touches on some of the themes of the "Switzerland" poems,
in particular "A Farewell" 33–36, 59–60.
    The connection with the "Marguerite" poems (and their basis
in experience) may account for the sporadic use of French in
entries 1 and 3. Cf. "The World's Triumphs."

[4]   This entry also suggests an emotional trauma. The kind of book A. has in mind is George Sand's *Jacques* (1834), full of her early characteristic "cry of agony and revolt," which A. recalled in his essay on the first anniversary of her death. (A.'s letter of 1845 to Clough recaptures his early enthusiastic response to *Jacques* [*CL*, 59].) The essay recalls

> Sylvia's cry over Jacques by his glacier in the Tyrol—"When such a man as thou art born into the world where he can do no true service[,] . . . the atmosphere suffocates him and he dies. . . . The world remains in all its vileness and in all its hatefulness; this is what men call, 'the triumph of good sense over enthusiasm.' " (*CPW*, 8:221; *Jacques*, sec. 95)

A.'s translation (and expansion) of "le triomph de la raison humaine" into "the triumph of good sense over enthusiasm" links this with entry 3. Jacques, who commits suicide amid Alpine glaciers, is somewhat akin to Obermann and to Empedocles on his fiery mountaintop.

Two or three years later, A. wrote to Clough in a vein similar to this entry, making explicit its link with the "loss of youth" theme so prominent in A.'s poetry (*CL*, 125).

The "suffocation" recalls "sich luft machen" (13r[2], p. 70).

[1]   So & so gives an opinion—how did he form it—penetrate yourself with the slight accidental way in wch A B C & D form & state opinions on all topics that do not vitally concern them, & do not in the deference to authority your own inward uncertainty eternaly° occasions in you, take their opinion for an absolute sentence—

[2]   —No man can express more than one side at once—τὸ οὖλον ἐπεύχεται εὑρεῖν° αὖτως—but he can have a feeling of the whole if he will not always be laboring after expression & publicity.

[3]   —All the keys* in you that have been struck upon will have rendered their sound: but no man leaves the universe having had every key† in him struck on, & having rendered every sound—

*"keys" replaced "stops."
†"key" replaced "stop."

[Aug., 1849/50]

[1]   The phrase "so and so" appears again in A.'s essay on "The
Literary Influence of Academies" (*CPW, 3:244*).

The comment may have been provoked by reading a review
of the recently published *Essay on the Influence of Authority in Matters of Opinion* (1849) by George Cornewall Lewis. The topic was
a popular one at the time, having been taken up by J. S. Mill,
Richard Whately, and William Whewall, among others, as well
as earlier, by Bacon, Locke, and Joseph Glanvill.

A. may be preaching to himself, but the comment is probably
aimed at the way in which the average Philistine forms his opinions, and so provides a link with facing page 5v[3] (p. 168).
Thirty years later, A. was even more scornful of Philistine public
opinion (*CPW, 9:148*).

[2]   A. is primarily concerned with achieving and then conveying
a sense of the whole, the All. He pursued the search both for
the sake of his own spiritual health and to satisfy his needs as
a poet. (Cf. *CL*, 97.)

The Greek is from fragment 2 of Empedocles' poem *On Nature,* quoted from *Empedoclis Agrigentini Carminum Reliquiae,* Karsten, 2:90. Karsten's Latin translation of the passage is:
"universum vero se perspexisse frustra quis gloriatur. . . ." Having noted the limitations of man's sensory experience, he observes that, nevertheless, "every man vainly boasts that he has
found the whole." (A. omitted "δὲ" [but], which follows "τὸ" in
the original. Cf. "Empedocles on Etna," I.ii.84–85, 341.) Karsten's commentary on the entire passage (translated) reads as
follows:

These verses, preserved by Sextus Empiricus, contain complaints about the brevity and wretchedness of life, about the
limitations of human understanding, about the misleading
evidences of the senses. Warnings are inserted that no one
should dare to be wise beyond the limit of human intellectual
ability or should trust the evidence of the senses. They who
boast that they know the force and nature of the universe are

rebuked. He implores the gods to bestow on him humility and wisdom. (2:171)

This must have been a favorite quotation, for A. refers to it familiarly, in very abbreviated fashion, in 13r[4] (p. 70). The last sentence refers to Empedocles' call to the gods to "avert my tongue from the madness of those men." (Cf. 1r[7], p. 57.) Empedocles deals not with the limitations imposed by expression but with the more fundamental limitation imposed by man's senses and his finite experience. These ideas find their clearest expression in "Empedocles on Etna," I.ii.82–85 and II.352–55.

A. commonly uses the word *expression* in two senses: either the entire process of making visible one's thoughts and feelings, or concern for striking individual images or lines, an excessive concern for parts rather than the total conception (*CPW*, 1:5, 7, 10). The context seems to indicate that A. has the first of these meanings in mind here, but the second is also implied.

In A.'s day, "publicity" was practically synonymous with expression, in the first sense—that is, the exposure of one's thoughts and feelings to the general public. (By the time of *Friendship's Garland* [1866–67], however, he begins to speak of false notions of liberty and publicity, linking them with an irresponsible press and dubbing them "clap trap" [*CPW*, 5:343, 353–55].)

For a different perspective on the conflict between thought and expression, see 3r[1], p. 154.

[3]   A. shifts his emphasis slightly, to focus on life rather than on expression—a shift already begun within entry 2. (Cf. 8r[5], p. 203, and A.'s later conception of "Hellenism," *CPW*, 5:235–36).

A. originally wrote "stops" instead of "keys," indicating some uncertainty about the operation of an organ. He may have recalled a sentence in Goethe's observations on "The Methods of French Criticism" (1817): "Here speaks an able, talented, intellectual man ... who, like the master of musical art, draws the stops of his well-equipped organ which express the thought and feeling of each moment" (Spingarn, 137; *Werke*, 14:783).

This page reveals several sides of A.'s concern with wholeness and suggests some of its roots and connections. All three entries touch upon some aspect of integration or totality.

[Sept., 1849/50]

See 13r[2–5], p. 70.

[2]   Indian Gazetter.
Then these infidels eat hog—then they drank wine: and then
they danced after their vile manner pulling about one
anothers' wives.

———

[1]   The easy tone of a Shakspeare suits the immoral vulgar: the
moralist conscious of his own imperfection & strain, admires
it: but what does the poet's own conscience say to it—what
would he say at seeing his easy morality erected by Germans &
others into a system of life, & a thing to be held in view as an
object for inward disciplining of oneself towards. He would
say—you fools—I have walked thro: life επι ξυρου ακμης God
knows how—if you mistake my razor edge, you damned
pedants, for a bridge, a nice mess you will make of your own
& others' walk & conversation.*

*See 6v[3] (p. 178) for entry completed at the bottom of this page.

[Sept., 1849/50]

[1]   "ἐπὶ ξυροῦ ἀκμῆς": on a razor's edge, from Nestor's speech rousing Diomede to action (*Iliad*, 10.173; A. omits accents). In a brief note to Clough, who was working on a translation of the *Iliad*, A. quotes the same phrase and adds, it "has not an English equivalent, literal, as you put it" (*CL*, 105, "about March, 1849").

In the last sentence, "walk" points back to "I have walked thro: life," but A. also has in mind its figurative and religious connotations, the "manner of behaviour, conduct of life" (*OED*). A. may also be harking back, unconsciously, to his childhood when, in and out of leg irons, the mere ability to walk with ease (and behave properly) were major concerns.

"[C]onversation" has an archaic sense roughly synonymous with "walk": "manner of conducting oneself in the world or in society; behaviour, mode or course of life" (*OED*). They probably constituted an idiom, for the *OED* quotes the same doublet from John Morley's essay on "Carlyle" (1878). A. seems to have the Authorized Version of the Bible in mind, perhaps reinforced by Carlyle's religious rhetoric. A. uses "conversation" twice more in this sense in the *YMS* (9r[4] and 4r[5], pp. 186 and 195). Cf. *N-Bs*, 126; April 2, 1870.

Rather than looking back to the sonnet on "Shakespeare" (1844), this entry points ahead to A.'s literary criticism in prose and his fascination with the subtle connections between literature and man's moral nature. "The easy tone of a Shakspeare" contrasts sharply with the censorious tone of the Indian commentator in entry 2, added later in ink to the penciled notebook entries.

[Aug., 1850/51]

[2]   "Gazetter": either a slip of the pen instead of "Gazetteer" or a neologism for one holding a military appointment announced in a gazette.

The entry consists of comments from an Indian point of view on a dinner and ball probably given by British officers. Examination of hundreds of gazetteers, books of travel, and periodicals has failed to turn up the source. A. was an enthusiastic reader of books on travel. His diary for 1853 includes "Macpherson's India" and "Schönberg's India"; and for 1854, "Hooker's Himalayan Journals" (*N-Bs*, 554–55). His interest in India increased when his brother William went out, in 1848, as a cadet in the Indian Army for the East India Company. William drew upon his experiences there for his novel *Oakfield* (1853) and may have quoted these comments in one of his letters for the amusement of the family.

[1]   We read to avoid the labour of an inward survey &
      arrangement—and are but heaping up more to be surveyed &
      arranged in some inevitable future. We cannot—cannot get
      breast to breast with a thought or a fact—we collect new
      specimens as a passe temps—but these too must be some day
      sorted.

[2]   —We have a fugitive delicate sense thro: wc̄h we know all
      things, & which needs only the slightest store* of facts &c: but
      this delicate sense is not in our own power & while it slumbers
      we load the more mechanical senses with occupation but can
      yet never feel right & in the centre of things. Ancient life may
      be felt on small knowledge of details: but we wade thro:
      volumes on Pompiei° & measure acres of ruins to get a
      succedaneum for this elusive feeling.

[3]   —the real central life is something exquisitely kind,

fine tempered, liberal, in good taste, unenvious comfortable in
itself.

*"store" replaced "suggestions."

[Sept. or Oct. 1849/50]

[1–2]   These entries seem to have been written during a period of
         depression, when A. felt keenly that reading can never become
         a substitute for thought, nor can perspiration replace inspira-
         tion. He was gathering information, but a synthesis, an "Idea of
         the world," seemed as far away as ever. (Cf. *CL*, 130–31 and
         136.)
              These reflections are intended to be dramatic as well as
         autobiographical. They reappear in "Empedocles on Etna,"
         I.ii.322–26, 332–35 and in ["The Second Best"], lines
         5, 14–15, 17–20 (3v, p. 194). Cf. 4v[3], p. 163.

[3]   The "central life" is much like "the buried life"—one's best or
         ideal or true self, usually inaccessible and, like the "delicate sense,"
         not in our own power.

[1]   What a thing it is to have a reason in oneself for doing or not doing a thing and how few have experienced it.

[2]   —every time we approach philosophy we test it by our hitherto acquired experience. It is better therefore to approach it late

[3]   —only that which recalls a whole can refresh him who looks upon a whole. Tennyson has the naiveté of language & image—but not the large plain manner of thinking & feeling that is in nature—the Greek philosophers (Epicurus Empedocles &c) have the great way of thinking, coextensive with nature, & not fantastically individual, but not the relief of the naiveté of Nature—with its landscapes & affections. Homer & the Old Testament & on the whole Shakspeare unite both.

[Oct., 1849/50]

[1]   The yearning for inner direction is part of A.'s Stoicism and
relates to his search for self-knowledge and to his call for "clear-
ness" in "A Summer Night," lines 76–77, and in "Courage," line
28. See pp. 23–25.

[2]   Cf. "Bishop Butler and the Zeit-Geist" (1877), *CPW*, 8:47.
     A. did not take his own advice, or gave the advice because he
realized the harmful consequences of not taking it. See *CL*,
136.

[Feb., 1850/51]

[3]   References in this entry help to date it. A.'s short list of Greek
philosophers here would seem unusual but for the fact that since
early in 1849 he had been working on "Empedocles on Etna."
He probably read Epicurus between March, 1849, and December, 1850 (almost certainly after Empedocles—see p. 74n). For
his reading of Homer, completed April–July, 1849 (and his enthusiasm for the literary qualities of the Bible), see *CL*, 103,
and *L*, July 29, 1849 (to his mother).
     Handwriting makes it likely that this entry was written after
he had read *In Memoriam* (ca. June, 1850).
     A. had a lifelong classical and humanistic concern for whole-
ness and harmony. The critical standards he enunciates here
point toward his distinction between "*natural magic*" and "*moral
profundity*" in his essay on "Maurice de Guérin" (*CPW*, 3:33).
See pp. 27–28. His stress on "the great way of thinking, coextensive with nature, & not fantastically individual" not only anticipates his concept of "high seriousness" but also his attacks on
English provinciality and the eccentricity it engendered. Cf.
CL, 72.

[1]   What is this I hear that no one feels the force of religious faith who has never doubted—that the inferiority of stoicism to Xtianity is never so clearly felt as by him who has exchanged the one religion for the other—it may be so but the convert has something else to do than to triumph over his past creeds, let him look for ever forwards to the ever deepening spreading Light of God on the horizon.

———

                          mutely

[2] — Snow-vested knolls that whitely slope
        Into
      Down to the glassy frozen tarns

———

[3]   That warm south scented & benignant breath
        man's
    that bathes our speech like moonlight

———

[4]   not the same mood befits
    The living & the dying—those who are to live must be vulgar like Napoleon—those who are to die may hang over Nature like Obermann.

———

[5]   some white soft-tissued cloud
    Floating under the thrond moon through heaven.

———

[6]   I believe
    That in the solitudes beyond the stars
    Where broods the uncompaniond life of God—

———

[7]   If to detect were always to retain—but whereas most men

have experiences & let them go, the superiority of the greatest minds is that they retain them, look at them

altogether, & learn* from them._____

*"learn" replaced "deduce."

[Oct., 1849/50]

[1]   A., at the time, was a "convert" from Christianity, but he cared
about religion and was groping toward faith. Compare "the ever
deepening spreading Light of God on the horizon" with "Dover
Beach," written less than two years later. See pp. 21ff.

[2, 3, 5]   "[B]enignant breath" (entry 3) reappears in "Euphrosyne"
(written shortly after August, 1850).
      These lines exemplify precisely the emphasis upon expres-
sion and detail that A. rejects in his 1853 preface to *Poems* in
favor of an "excellent action" and concern for the whole. Although their emotional tone is calm and "consoling," in Arnoldian terms, all three unrhymed pairs of verses emphasize imagery
and manipulate sound in an almost Tennysonian way.

[6]   What primarily sets these lines apart from the others is the
absence of sensory imagery. The image of the "life of God" is at
odds with most of the assumptions about the nature of God in
the *YMS*.

[4]   "The living & the dying" can best be understood through
"Stanzas in Memory of the Author of 'Obermann,'" written not
long before. Active men of the world are "the living"; those who
have withdrawn from active participation for the sake of con-
templation and meditation (as in A.'s poems on monastic life)
are "the dying." This passage points toward the paradox that
only the dying can remain in harmony with nature. The price
of life in the world is alienation from her. Achieving a delicate
balance between involvement and detachment was always a particularly acute problem for the poet and critic in A.
      A.'s attack on the Philistines and his emphasis upon disinter-
estedness in "The Function of Criticism at the Present Time"
have some of their roots in this passage. (See commentary on
4r[5], p. 198.)
      For A.'s appreciation of Napoleon, see letter to his mother,
May 7, 1849° (*L;* cf. 9r[3], p. 186). Napoleon is "vulgar" primarily in the sense that he is of the common people and a man

of practical affairs, but A. also sensed a coarse, common element in him, as in Byron.

[7]   This comment is consonant not only with A.'s belief that art must be grounded in experience (5r[3], p. 165) but also with his emphasis upon the function of memory (31r[1], p. 109) and the all-importance of achieving a sense of wholeness.

[Oct., 1849/50]

See 12v[2–3] (p. 128).

[1]* our remotest self must abide in its remoteness awful & unchanged, presiding at the tumult of the rest of our being, changing thoughts contending desires &c as the moon over the agitations of the Sea.

———

[2] —We are plunged at birth into a boundless sea, crystal clear, where all may be seen as the eye gets accustomed to the watery medium thro: wc̄h it is to look—but we are agitated & alarmed & by our strugles° trouble the transparent medium, & die having seen nothing.

———

[3] The Spirit of *Life* pours itself into this or that man, & the power and vivacity of his operations make the feeble ghostlike mass of mankind adore him, & follow his oracles as if the Spirit of *Truth* had dictated them: but it is not so: Caesar,† Goethe, Napoleon are mightily enstrengthened by the indwelling Spirit of *Life:* but the Spirit of *Truth* incarnates itself seldom‡ or never in man§. If ever, in the still & hardly known.

[4] —To desire to be *natural* in conversation, & not to have the *force* necessary to supply the demands this desire makes on your collectedness invention & spirit.

———

[5] —It is so—all# are born to feel—some to

express—tho: every feeling has its word, every one who has the feeling cannot seize the word: and yet we live in a time when expression is so universal & appears so facile that all who have the feeling imagine they can find the expression too—but it is not so.

*At the top of the page is the conclusion of 8v[7]. See pp. 182–83.
†Written in ink over "Wordsworth."
‡Written over "never."
§"in man" added.
#Written over "some."

[Oct., 1849/50]

All these pessimistic entries deal with man and his environment. They usually assume the existence of two modes or levels of being.

[1]   Cf. the early sonnet "Written in Butler's Sermons" and the relatively late "Palladium." The "remotest self" is akin to "the buried life." For "the tumult . . . of our being," see 2r (p. 145).

[2]   This is a version of the Fall described in terms of loss of vision. Goethe, in A.'s 1848 translation of "Für junge Dichter," refers to the forces that "trouble the clear spring" (unpublished 1847 notebook, fol. 39; *Werke* [L.H.], 45:424; *Werke*, 14:401, where it is entitled "Wohlgemeinte Erwiderung"). In "Empedocles on Etna," I.ii.204–5, A. applies this image to those who hold to what is false. Cf. Goethe's image of entanglement (1r[8], p. 57). In "Stanzas in Memory of the Author of 'Obermann,' " lines 61–62, 83–84, A. draws upon both images in referring to Goethe. The association between alarm and struggle reappears in "Dover Beach," line 36, transferred from sea to land.

[3]   "oracles": "infallible guide[s]" (*OED*). Cf. A.'s ironic reference to his early poems both as lacking "a consistent meaning" and as "oracles" (letter to "K," Mar., 1849°; *UL*, 18–19). He also refers to "A Caution to Poets," 9v[3] (p. 189), as an "oracular quatrain," *CL*, 126. (For a discussion of A.'s "Voice Oracular," see Johnson, *Voices of Matthew Arnold*, 11–40.)
       A. is less concerned with debunking great men (he deliberately selected those who fascinated him most) than with bringing out human limitations. (See letter to his mother, May 7, 1849,° in *L*.) Faced with a choice between a life of action and the detached life of a writer, A. doubts the possibility of attaining ultimate wisdom in either direction. See pp. 19–20.

[4]   "conversation": behavior. Cf. 7r[1] and 4r[5] (pp. 175 and 195).

If it is unrealistic to hope to achieve Truth, one may at least try to be natural, expressing "the simple feelings of humanity. . . . with the most perfect limpidity" (5r[3], p. 165), but even that is difficult. A.'s concern with naturalness is part of his attempt to find himself and be himself, and to achieve self-mastery.

[5]   This connects the problem of being natural with the problem of expression. (Cf. *CL*, 98–99.) A.'s translation of Goethe's "Für junge Dichter" begins:

> Our Language has attained so high a Pitch of cultivation, that it is possible for every one . . . to express himself happily in conformity with his object or his feeling, according to his ability. Hence it follows, that everyone who by hearing & reading has cultivated himself up to a certain point, at which he is in some degree clear to himself, immediately feels himself impelled to communicate his thoughts & judgements, his perceptions & feelings with a certain ease & facility.—But it is hard, almost impossible for the young to see, that by this nothing has been done in the higher sense. (Unpublished 1847 notebook, fols. 37–38; *Werke* [L.H.], 45:423–24; *Werke*, 14:400, entitled "Wohlgemeinte Erwiderung")

For Goethe, facile expression leads to superficial, solipsistic poetry; for A., it demonstrates the difficulty of using language with precision, especially to express feelings. Only fine writers really understand the difficulty of writing well and the impossibility of finding precise verbal equivalents for their vision. Cf. 5v[1], p. 168.

[1]*   Our present condition with its progress, backslidings,
        experiences &c is so insignificant that we willingly push it out
        of mind afin de go to meet some better thing in the world
        without us, in books, society, news, &c &c. But every man's
        self is an unshakeoffable poor-relation whom he may go into
        no new sphere without taking with him.

[2]   The Christians introduced the word humility where the
        Greeks had used moderation.

[3]   —What it gave us no pleasure to conceive or make it will give
        the world no pleasure to contemplate

            What poets feel not when they make
            A pleasure in creating
            The world in *its* turn will not take
            Pleasure in contemplating.

[4]   —The Spirit of the world enounces the problems

        which this or that generation of men is to work: men do not
        fix them for themselves. Those who attempt to enounce &
        work their own have the fate of all intempestive things—they
        perish.

[5]   —When Spinoza, arguing agˢt the doctrine of final causes
        says—God did not make the world for man's sake, because if
        he did, he worked propter finem, & qui propter finem agit
        aliquid necessario appetit quo caret; for he could not strictly
        have worked propter res creandas before creation, and must
        therefore have worked propter &c, and therefore caruisse
        aliquo, et id cupivisse, which is a mark of imperfection, he
        argues like a schoolman not like himself.

---

*At the top of the page is the conclusion of 9r[5]. See p. 186.

[Nov., 1849/50]

[1]   See *CL*, 111, September 23, 1849. Cf. 6v[1] (p. 178) on reading and piling up information as escapist activities.

The self as "unshakeoffable poor-relation" is our "ordinary" social self. See pp. 15–16.

[2]   The contrast between Christian and Greek ideals points toward "Pagan and Mediaeval Religious Sentiment" (1863) and also toward such pairings as Hebraism and Hellenism in *Culture and Anarchy.*

["The Second Best"] (3v–4r, pp. 194–95) presents an un-Hellenic form of moderation.

[3]   A. quoted this poem (later entitled "A Caution to Poets") in a letter to Clough, December 14, 1852, apropos of the lack of charm in his own second volume of poems (*CL*, 126), but he did not publish the quatrain until 1867. The entry is a negative version of Goethe's comment in "Antik und Modern": "every work will afford us pleasure [*Freude*] which the artist himself produced with ease and facility" (Spingarn, 67; *Werke*, 13:843; see *P*, 301n). Cf. 5r[4] (p. 165), where A. notes that one's work reflects the quality and scope of one's life.

[4]   "The Spirit of the world" is another name for the Time-Spirit, or *Zeitgeist*—a word that A. borrowed from Goethe and Carlyle.

This entry reflects A.'s Stoic belief in the necessity of submitting to the universal order. See p. 11.

[Feb., 1850/51]

[5]   A. is commenting upon the following passage from Spinoza:

Deinde haec doctrina Dei perfectionem tollit: Nam, si Deus propter finem agit, aliquid necessario appetit, quo caret. Et quamvis Theologi et Metaphysici, distinguant inter finem indigentiae et finem assimilationis, fatentur tamen, Deum omnia propter se, non vero propter res creandas egisse; quia

nihil ante creationem praeter Deum assignare possunt, propter quod Deus ageret; adeoque necessario fateri, coguntur,
Deum iis, propter quae media parare voluit, caruisse, eaque
cupivisse, ut per se clarum. (Spinoza, *Opera,* 1:69)

... this doctrine destroys the perfection of God: for if God
seeks an end, he necessarily desires something which he lacks.
And although theologians and metaphysicians make a distinction between the end that is want and that which is assim-
ilation, they confess that God acts on his own account, and
not for the sake of creating things; for before the creation
they can assign nothing save God on whose account God
acted, and so necessarily they are obliged to confess that God
lacked and desired those things for the attainment of which
he wished to prepare means, as is clear of itself. (Spinoza,
Ethics [Everyman], pt. 1, app., 33.)

A. probably read the first parts of the *Ethics* in 1850. (See p.
62 n. 2) He came to Spinoza through Goethe at a time when
a revival of interest in Spinoza was already under way at Oxford.

a God identical with the world and with the sum of being &
force therein contained: not exterior to it, possessing being &
force exterior to it, and determining it à son gré.

[1850]

"à son gré": at his pleasure, as he pleases.

This definition, so far as it goes, best expresses A.'s view of God at the time. The closest A. comes to expressing this point of view explicitly in his poetry is in "Empedocles on Etna," I.ii.287–301.

There is probably no single source for this entry. Empedocles, the Stoics, the Bhagavad-Gita, Spinoza, Goethe, Emerson, and others may all have contributed. (See Allott, "Empedocles," *E & S*, n.s., 21[1968]: 93.)

[1850]

See 1r[5–6] (p. 57).

[Feb., 1850/51]

See 1r[7–8] (p. 57).

[1]

1 Moderate tasks & moderate leisure
2 Quiet living strict kept measure
3 Both* in suffering and in pleasure—
4 'Tis for this thy nature yearns.

5 But so many books thou readest
   such anxious
6 But so many schemes thou breedest
   such furious
7 But so many passions feedest—
8 That thy poor head almost turns.

9 And (the world's so madly jangled,
10 Human things so deep entangled°
11 Nature's wish must now be strangled
12 For that best which she discerns

   ───

13 So it must be—yet, while leading
14 A strain'd life, while over-feeding
15 Like the rest, his wit with reading
16 No small profit that man earns

   ───

17 Who from history's vague narrations,
18 From pretentious teas'd relations
19 Of man's mental operations
20 Turning sick & baffled learns

*Written over "Tis."

194

[2] We know our history since we woke on earth—
     But ere we woke, we were—

21 That the one lore that's assuring
22 Is "Persistance° all-enduring—"
23 That man's spirit at its luring
24 Deeply stirs & truly burns.

[3] The coldness & dissatisfaction of men in presence of our
     works is an indication that we have not yet reached perfection
     in working: their coldness & dissatisfaction in presence of
     ourselves, that we have not yet reached it in behaviour. ——

[4] —We lie outstretched on a vast wave of the starlit sea of life,
     balancing backwards & forwards with it: we desire the shore,
     but we shall reach it only when our wave reaches it.

[5] —We may be the only wise & just beings in the world: then
     périssons en resistant° & let our conversation be an eternal
     reproach to the immorality of the world that contains us.

[6] No [?] observes the growth or the decay   they that[?] tell
     —the triste [?] & mechanical life of the world-conquered.

[Feb., 1850/51]

[1]   Published in *Empedocles on Etna* (Oct., 1852) under the title
"The Second Best." A. kept reprinting the poem from 1867 on,
but he acknowledged its limitations by placing it among his "Early
Poems," despite the date of its composition.

Aside from punctuation and spelling, A. made the following
changes:

Line 6: adopted "so many schemes," the first reading;
Line 7: "such furious passions" became "so many wishes";
Line 13: italicized "must" (beginning in 1867).

A. completely rewrote the last two stanzas, except for the first
and last words of the first stanza and the first and last four words
of the second stanza:

17 Who through all he meets can steer him,
18 Can reject what cannot clear him,
19 Cling to what can truly cheer him;
20   Who each day more surely learns

21 That an impulse, from the distance
22 Of his deepest, best existence,
23 To the words, 'Hope, Light, Persistence,'
24   Strongly stirs and truly burns.

The word *its* (line 23 of entry 1) refers not to "man's spirit"
but to "the one lore" (i.e., "Persistance"), as the revised conclusion makes clear. "[S]tirs" (line 24) became "sets" in 1869.

Despite the fact that entry 2, at the top of sheet 4r, separates
the last stanza from the first five stanzas, handwriting indicates
that A. wrote the poem without a break, adding entry 2 later.
The final stanza continues the sentence in stanza 4.

The moderation that the speaker seeks owes little or nothing
to A.'s favorite concept from Aristotle's *Nichomachean Ethics*. It
owes rather more to Plato's concept of *sophrosyne:* self-control,
moderation, temperance. But in essence the poem is unchar-
acteristically Neoclassical in outlook. It sounds more like what

an eighteenth-century Empedocles would prescribe for an Augustan Pausanias than something A. considered valid.

Handwriting links entry 2 much more closely to 3 than it does to "The Second Best."

[2]   This entry led to lines 3 and 4 of "Self-Deception" (published 1852):

> —Since man woke on earth, he knows his story,
> But, before we woke on earth, we were.

In the context of the poem, it is clear that A. had in mind book 10 of *The Republic*, where Plato posits an existence that precedes life on earth. A., of course, altered the myth. (See Bonnerot, *Matthew Arnold, Poète*, 165n, and *P*, 292n. Wordsworth made very different use of the myth in his "Immortality" ode.) In its emphasis upon human limitations, the poem reinforces the pessimism of "The Second Best."

[3]   The pursuit of perfection was a lifelong preoccupation that became more insistent as A. turned to prose (cf. 20r, p. 207); but the idea of measuring one's achievement by the reaction of others is unusual in A. This uncharacteristic entry stems from one of the most stressful periods in his life involving a difficult courtship and dissatisfaction with the poetry he had written.

[4]   This entry has something in common with "Human Life" (stanzas 2 and 3), "Sohrab and Rustum," lines 390–97, and A.'s letter to Clough of October 10, 1853 (*CL*, 144). There are also connections with "Dover Beach" (sea, waves, night scene), but the symbolism of land and sea are reversed. Entry 2 (3r, p. 154) points to the next stage and man's unwillingness to rest content.

These examples reveal that A. resisted establishing a rigid pattern of symbolic equivalences despite his frequent use of a relatively small number of metaphorical vehicles. He constantly shifts man's position among such variables as land and water, regarding them now as goal and then as something to be shunned. In these early years, A. instinctively used metaphor as a means of conceptualizing and confronting his problems.

[5]   "conversation": behavior, way of life (cf. 7r[1] and 9r[4], pp. 175 and 186).

Senancour, *Obermann:* "c'est de nos fortes résolutions que quelque effet subsistera peut-être.—L'homme est périssable.— Il se peut; mais périssons en résistant, et, si le néant nous est réservé, ne faisons pas que ce soit une justice" (letter 90; Michaut, 2:231). ("If anything is abiding it will be the outcome of our firm resolutions. 'Man is perishable,' is the response. That may be; but let us perish resisting, and if annihilation must be our portion, let us not make it a just one" [Barnes, 2:252].)

A. drew upon this passage again in "The Function of Criticism at the Present Time" (*CPW*, 3:276). In both, A. turns *Obermann* to his own uses.

[6]   The handwriting of this sentence is the most difficult to decipher in the *YMS*, because it is squeezed in at the bottom of the page, is written in haste with some erasing, and includes three words, "they that[?] tell," apparently part of an earlier note.

Those leading "mechanical" lives have abandoned the struggle to realize their best selves or even to be true to themselves. Compare the "world-conquered" with the "slaves" of "A Summer Night," lines 37–50, 75. (Cf. *CL*, 109ff., where A. quotes from his own "Obermann" stanzas with their reference to "The Children of the Second Birth / Whom the world could not tame . . . ." See also commentary on 1r, p. 61.)

[1]   The Germans are so little in the full stream of life that they
      have full time to analyse and name all the filets d'eau that
      come past them: hence the singular *appuyering* character of
      their language: hence also the ridiculous figure they cut to an
      English or French eye. A German borne by the stream as
      almost every one in France & England is is hard to imagine
      even. Even in Goethe his language of freedom and head
      above water feeling in his theatrum mundi at Weimar seems
      astonishing to people used to think of a little German court as
      a hen coop. But man has limited faculties & very little from
      without is sufficient fully to employ them. Those are happiest
      in whom the equilibrium between the supply & the receptive
      power is best maintained: for whom the events of their daily
      life do not too much preponderate over their absorbent &
      regulant powers. Yet do not fail to remark the bad side of this
      equilibrium in the German character & language. Man
      perverts everything.

[2]   —I praise thee, O God that thou hast created me—My Life
      became at the last, thro: thy goodness, full of peace. O God
      shut not my soul out from thy divine presence. Lead me, O
      merciful Father, to the life of life.   (Esther's tomb)

[3]   —Why are we so interested in origines,° and in the dark ages.
      Because man had in one case not overexcited himself—& in
      the other had succeeded in forgetting—had thrown off

      the burden of his over-stimulated, sophisticated, artificialized
      false-developed miserable nervous sceptical self, and begun
      life anew. To this the race when over-cultivated tends, and
      does now tend, & did tend in the Roman times.

[Feb., 1850/51]

[1]   "filets d'eau": rivulets.

"appuyering": supporting (a coinage; a French verb with an English suffix).

"theatrum mundi": world theater, theater of mankind.

The phrase "head above water feeling" has its counterpart in A.'s unpublished letter of May 11, [1850], to his sister "K," where A. writes about "the necessity of somehow getting my head above the present English atmosphere"—followed by a reference to Goethe (in the Balliol College Library, Oxford). Similarly, in a letter to Clough, he seeks to avoid being "sucked for an hour even into the Time Stream" (*CL*, 95, Nov. 29, 1849°).

By the time of *On Translating Homer* (1861), instead of seeing the German language as providing buoyancy, he describes it as heavy (*CPW*, 1:101).

In writing of "the equilibrium between the supply & the receptive power," A. is thinking primarily of poets. (Cf. *CL*, 99. The entire letter throws light on this entry.)

[2]   This is an abridgment and improvement upon a translation of the Hebrew inscription that runs around the upper ledge of the sarcophagus in which the biblical Esther (second quarter, fifth century B.C.) is supposedly buried—quoted from Sir Robert Porter's *Travels*. The two large quarto volumes are profusely illustrated by their author, who translated into English a Persian translation of the Hebrew:

> *I praise thee, O God, that thou hast created me!* I know that my sins merit punishment, yet I hope for mercy at thy hands; for whenever I call upon thee, thou art with me; thy holy presence secures me from all evil.
>
> My heart is at ease, and my fear of thee increases. *My life became, through thy goodness, at the last full of peace.*
>
> *O God! do not shut my soul out from thy divine presence!* Those whom thou lovest, never feel the torments of hell. *Lead me, O merciful Father, to the life of life;* that I may be filled with the

heavenly fruits of paradise!—Esther. (2:111, emphasis added)

The tombs of Esther, legendary second wife of Ahasuerus (called Xerxes by the Greeks), and her cousin Mordecai are at Hamadan, Iran (formerly Ecbatana, Persia, once the capital of Media). The original building housing the sepulchres is said to have been destroyed by Timour (Tamerlane). Porter eulogizes Esther as "one of the most lovely pictures of female perfection."

A. was fascinated by books of travel and often drew on them for the background of his poetry.

He makes use of the phrase "the life of life" in "Empedocles on Etna," II.357. Empedocles seeks to pierce the "stifling veils" of the senses and embrace the All, the universal order of nature. Both the inscription and Empedocles use the phrase to refer to the highest goal of man, but one puts it in the framework of participation in the joys of heaven and the other in terms of participation in the cosmic process.

[3]   "origines": origins, sources, beginnings, roots. A. uses the French word because he has in mind a subject of historical research: "What the French call the *science des origines,* the science of origins,—a science which is at the bottom of all real knowledge of the actual world, and which is every day growing in interest and importance . . ." (*On the Study of Celtic Literature* [1867], *CPW,* 3:299). A. defines science here as "knowing things as they are." Later in the same work, he speaks of the science of origins as "teaching us which way our natural affinities and repulsions lie" (3:301; for A.'s interest in "affinities" see p. 18). A. also refers to "the science or origins" in reviewing A. W. Ward's translation of Ernst Curtius, *The History of Greece* (*CPW,* 5:260). Among the works that A. read in the 1840s dealing with "origines" were Jules Michelet, *Histoire de France,* volume 1 (1833), the Marquis de Bouillé's *Mémoires sur la révolution française depuis son origine . . .* (1801), and the third book of Bishop Stillingfleet's *Origines Sacrae, or a Rational Account of the Grounds of Christian Faith* (1662). In 1845, he began reading *Aegyptens Stelle in der Weltgeschichte* by Chevalier von Bunsen. Its introduc-

tion contains many references to the study of "origines." The biblical world of Esther and the ancient Persian empire were, of course, part of the "origines" that so interested A.

A. planned to deal with all these topics in "Lucretius," and he did deal with them in "Empedocles on Etna." In "The Scholar-Gipsy" he explores almost every characteristic that this entry attributes to the modern world.

[1]* —you must plunge yourself down to the depths of the sea of intuition: all other men are trying as far as lies in them to keep you on the barren surface.

[2] —The present state of the human race, state of language† public opinion, institutions &c, are in great measure the result of accident: yet in the human race is a power superior to accident, with the bent to shape all it comes in contact with to its own ideal rule.

[3] —nature complains that man directly he is sevré forgets her— that his conquests do her no pleasure.

[4] Job—22. 2.3.

[5] —human nature is unspeakably ductile—all it is steadily directed to it will become or perform: only it refuses to be two things at once—when trained to this it will not also be that. G. & S. in their correspondence & self-management make themselves what their reason prescribes: but for that very reason they are not what the great free-operating poets Shakspeare or Molière, are.

[6] —Thou beholdest George Sand, Musset, Bulwer, Jacobi &c, and wishest to get out & uttered like them, even though like most of them in a false strain—but never—

*The page begins with the conclusion of 7v[3]. See p. 199.
†"state of language" added.

[Feb., 1850/51]

[1]   A. combines here in an unusual way two common features of
his writing: the idea of two levels of existence and the sea as
symbol. Cf. "The Buried Life," "Empedocles on Etna," II.371
and I.ii.130, and "The Youth of Man," line 118. The closest
equivalent to "the sea of intuition" appears in "The Forsaken
Merman."

[2]   This entry also implies two levels, but here the focus is on
public rather than private life. "[A]ccident" is the result of men
acting mechanically "on the barren surface." An "ideal rule" can
come only from the depths of their being, from their best selves.

[3–4]   "sevré": weaned.
         Job 22:2–3: "Can a man be profitable unto God, as he that
is wise may be profitable unto himself? Is it any pleasure to the
Almighty, that thou art righteous? Or is it gain to him, that thou
makest thy ways perfect?"
         Job was one of A.'s favorite books. These rhetorical questions
imply a negative answer; yet God does take pleasure in Job. A.,
however, probably wanted to focus on these two verses. He makes
no attempt to resolve the conflict between entries 3 and 4. It
is significant that A. placed these entries in the midst of comments on how to live. Obviously, even in these years he never
quite lost the sense that man was part of the natural order—and
even more, that God or nature cared about what men did with
their lives.

[5]   The several strands here do not form a logical chain; instead,
they reflect A.'s musings on the contradictory elements of human nature and human achievement.

         a. Man is malleable.
         b. Mastery can be achieved only at the price of limitation, of
            being only one thing at a time (cf. 3r[3] and 6r[2–3],
            pp. 154 and 171, and the letter to "K" of Jan. 25,
            1851 [L]). Major poems deal with "refusal of limitation"
            (25r–v).

    c. Goethe and Schiller ("G. & S.") illustrate what can be achieved through reason. On November 15, 1796, Goethe wrote to Schiller from Weimar: "after our mad venture with the *Xenia* we must now devote ourselves exclusively to great and important works of art, and, to the confusion of all our adversaries, transmute our Protean nature into forms that are noble and good" (*Correspondence*, trans. Schmitz, 1:257; *Werke*, 20:272).

    d. Goethe and Schiller, despite A.'s admiration for them, differ from the very greatest creative geniuses like Shakespeare and Molière, who are pragmatists rather than ideologues or, in words A. later applied to the ideal critic, they are "ondoyant et divers" (*CPW*, 1:174).

[6]   By "uttered" A. may have meant something like "have your meaning expressed" or "be able to express yourself."

    A. writes here in a "false strain," a kind of broken Carlylese. Note the odd shift of tense in "uttered," the biblical flavor of the second person singular, the "ever . . . never" contrast, and the ending suggesting "but you never will succeed even in this."

    George Sand (1804–76), A.'s favorite novelist during his Oxford years, opened up to him a new world of feeling and freedom. By the late forties, her magic spell over him was beginning to weaken. See A.'s essay on her (*CPW*, 8:216–36).

    Alfred de Musset (1810–57) was A.'s favorite among the French romantic poets. A. probably first read him in the pages of the *RDM* and later owned a collection of his poems. He was also a novelist and dramatist, as well as lover of George Sand in the early thirties. A. considered his poetry inferior to Wordsworth's but superior to Tennyson's (*CL*, 154, Mar. 9, 1861). From about January 17 to February 10, 1851, A. read his *La confession d'un enfant du siècle* (A.'s unpublished 1851 diary).

    Edward G. E. L. Bulwer-Lytton (1803–73), was a prolific popular novelist as well as dramatist, poet, and politican. A. discussed him with George Sand when he met her at Nohant in 1846 (*CPW*, 8:218).

    Friedrich Heinrich Jacobi (1743–1819), novelist, philosopher, and academician, was neither a professional creative writer like the others nor one of their generation. A. probably included him because he had recently been reading his correspondence with Goethe, published in 1846 (*CL*, 116, Oct. 23, 1850).

A. seems to have listed these writers in descending order of merit, with only George Sand (usually) and Musset (at times) exempted from the "false strain." As older contemporaries, they belonged to the generation of writers whom A. would normally have been expected to emulate, but A. considered all contemporaries bad models. They lacked perspective as guides through the maze of the present, being too caught up in the "over-cultivated" world he describes in 7v[3] (p. 199). Moreover, A. regarded any direct imitation of the manner of a writer as misguided. In an early letter to Clough (ca. 1845), he insists: "Rightly considered, a Code-G.-Sand would make G. Sands impossible" (*CL*, 59). Besides, "the form generally should change with each new matter" (5r[4]–4v, p. 165).

Throughout these entries a dialectic is at work, juxtaposing historical periods, levels of human nature, kinds of faculties, and types of achievement.

[Mar., 1850/51]

See 13r[6] p. 70.

Le perfectionnement exige un travail continu, souvent ingrat,
et qu'il faut sans cesse renouveler, en vous proposant ce but
sublime d'être en terminant votre carrière un peu meilleur
que vous n'etiez° en la commençant.

90

[Aug., 1850/51]

"Perfection requires sustained, often thankless effort, and it must be ceaselessly renewed if you are to pursue this lofty goal: to end your life a little better than you began it." (Source unidentified.)

The pursuit of perfection, with its roots in Greek and Stoic sources, is central to A.'s idea of culture and criticism.

_____

Then wilt thou learn if not
The clue to happiness
At least that Gods thy lot
Single not for distress

thwart   welfare
That Natural causes mar thy efforts & not fate.

That each man's lot is that
Which he can win or keep
Nor does Heaven toil thereat
To make him laugh or weep:
Learn that men will not & gods cannot help thy state.

_____

[Oct., 1850/51]

Form as well as content indicates that these stanzas were once meant as part of Empedocles' address to Pausanias, "Empedocles on Etna," I.ii. They form a unit, as can be seen from their subject matter, their parallel structure, and the fact that their concluding hexameters rhyme. No single stanza or pair of stanzas replaces them in the published version, but the ideas they express can be found throughout Empedocles' homily, especially I.ii. 147–76, 257–81, and 304–16.

The use of hexameters to conclude each stanza conveys a little of the flavor of Lucretius' *De Rerum Natura* (A.'s model) and of Empedocles. A.'s sparing use of hexameters may have been influenced by his dislike for Clough's *Bothie* (1848), written entirely in hexameters.

For the Epicurean view of the gods, see Lucretius, *De Rerum Natura* 2:174ff., 646ff., and 5:155ff. Cf. "Mycerinus," lines 19–54 and "The Strayed Reveller," lines 130ff. In the final version of "Empedocles on Etna," it is Nature rather than the Epicurean gods who is indifferent to man (I.ii.257ff.). The Gods are simply scapegoats invented by man (I.ii.277–305).

The first two lines of the second stanza are indebted to two of A.'s comments in prose—a sentence from Ashley Library A17 1r (quoted on p. 87) and 37v^2[9] (p. 84).

Lines 3 and 4 of both stanzas share the outlook of a passage from Goethe's *Dichtung und Wahrheit*, book 2, that A. translated (June, 1847–48) into his General Notebook 1, under the heading "The Same" ["School Bullying"]: "man experiences how it has gone with others, and what he too has to expect from life: and . . . that this happens to him as man and not as a peculiarly favoured or spited Being" (*N-Bs*, 448; *Werke* [L.H.], 24:104; *Werke*, 10:78).

[Feb., 1852/53]

See 3r[3] (p. 154).

The first page of the last entry in the Yale Manuscript.

[3]   Caesar like Cromwell
 [a] ne point s'associer à la politique ni à la destinée de ces
     institutions et de ces hommes; se tenir en dehors de leurs
 [b] fautes et de leur° revers—grandir pendent que d'autres
 [c] s'usaient.
   62

     Les grandes hommes d'action ne construisent point
     d'avance et de toutes pièces leur plan de conduite. Leur génie
     est dans leur instinct et dans leur ambition. *Chaque jour, dans*
 [d] *chaque circonstance, ils voient les faits tels qu'ils sont reellement.*° Ils
     marchent à la dictature sans bien savoir où ils arriveront, ni à
     quel prix: mais ils marchent toujours.

[4]   — Caesar on the patricians who want to be rulers and masters
     per saltum without trouble, by right of birth.

[5]   — Dio* on Caesar's want of *Halt*—(divorces debauchery &c)

[6]   The *point of view*   everything—every one bourgeois and

[1]   The deep-brow'd oaks philister, whatever his manners or

                              acquirements, who has not this,

[2]   For man woud° ask no questions where his wish obeyed

[7]   Caesar on death in Sallust. Drumann. Caesar. 749.

*Written over "Dion."

These entries all relate to A.'s unfinished drama "Lucretius." The first two, in pencil, belong to an early stage, when material for it was being incorporated into "Empedocles on Etna." (See "chew Lucretius" under the heading "Comp.—1849," 25r[2], p. 114.) The others are much later and involve Caesar, who was to have had an important role in the play. Unlike the material in the notebook that H. F. Lowry entitled "Mythologica" and that contains, with much else, notes on Caesar's public career, these entries reveal something of his character, outlook, and values, and are the stuff out of which dramatic speeches could have been made.

[Feb., 1849/50]

[1]   A. frequently begins poems with descriptions that project the human situation.

[2]   A. incorporated into Empedocles' advice to Pausanias a variant of this hexameter—"For man would make no murmuring, were his will obeyed" ("Empedocles on Etna," I.ii.151; for the probable influence of Carlyle and Epictetus, see *P*, 171n).

[Mar., 1856/57]

[3]   A. condensed and altered a passage (pp. 62–63) from François Guizot, *Pourquoi la révolution d'Angleterre a-t-elle réussi? Discours sur l'histoire de la révolution d'Angleterre* (*Why Was the English Revolution Successful? A Discourse on the History of the English Revolution*). Entry 3r[3] (p. 154) contains the only explicit cross-reference in the *YMS*, a reference to page 62 of this pamphlet.

    Guizot relates how once the destructive phase of the revolution had been concluded, Cromwell sought to stand apart from his fellow revolutionaries in the new Parliament in order to establish an independent base for the constructive phase of the revolution—the task at which he failed: that of reshaping his country's institutions. The passage is translated as follows.

    [One resolve ... occupied the thoughts of Cromwell:] to dissociate himself from the policy and destiny of these insti-

tutions and these men; to keep aloof from their faults and
their reverses—to grow in strength and renown, while others
were working their own ruin.

Men whose greatness lies in action do not lay far-reaching
and elaborate plans of conduct. Their genius lies in their in-
stinct and their ambition. *From day to day, in each circumstance
as it occurs, they see facts as they really are.* They advance toward
the dictatorship without clearly knowing whither they are
going, or at what cost; but onward still they go. (Based upon
the translations of William Hazlitt [1850], 27, and Mrs. Austin [1850], 46.)

A. made the following changes and omissions (noted in
brackets):

a. The first sentence began: "[Une pensée préoccupa dès lors
   Cromwell:] ne point . . . ."
b. "de leurs revers[; se séparer du parlement en le servant.
      C'était peu de se séparer; il fallait] grandir . . . ."
c. "s'usaient. [Cromwell prévoyait la ruine du parlement et
   de ces chefs; décidé à ne pas tomber avec eux, il voulait
   s'élever à coté d'eux.]"
d. "réellement. [Ils entrevoient le chemin que ces faits leur
   indiquent et les chances que ce chemin leur ouvre.] Ils [y
   entrent vivement, et y] marchent[, toujours à la même lu-
   mière et aussi loin que l'espace s'ouvre devant eux. Cromwell marchait] à la dictature sans bien savoir où [il
   arriverait], ni à quel prix; mais [il marchait] toujours."

A. later incorporated the notion of "seeing things as they
really are" (underlined) into the definition of several of his
key concepts—"culture," "criticism," and "Hellenism" (*CPW*,
1:140; 3:258; 5:97, 167 and passim). A characteristic of the
man of action became the hallmark of the disinterested ob-
server's best self.

Carlyle probably kindled A.'s interest in Cromwell, the assigned subject of A.'s Newdigate Prize poem. Several historians
with whose works A. was familiar had already noted similarities

between Caesar and Cromwell, among them F.-A.-M Mignet, B. G. Niebuhr, and Theodor Mommsen. It is unlikely, however, that A. had yet read Mommsen on Caesar, for their interpretations differ markedly on just those features that mattered most to A.

[4]   "per saltum": at a leap or bound, equivalent to "at once"— not an idiom in classical Latin. Bernard Shaw, surprisingly, uses it in his preface to *Major Barbara* (*Collected Plays*, 3:31).

There is no record of Caesar having uttered these words, so they must be A.'s invention. They do, however, correctly express Caesar's views. The patricians had lost much of their political influence even before Caesar came to power.

[5]   "Dio": Cassius Dio Cocceianus, generally referred to as Dion Cassius or Cassius Dio (ca. A.D. 150–235). A.'s pocket diary for December 1, 1856, lists, among others, "Date of . . . Dion Cassius." Less than twenty volumes of his eighty-volume *Roman History* survive intact. It covered the entire range of Roman history from its origins until his own day. Twice consul, he shows increasing political insight as his history approaches his own times. Dr. Arnold had a very low opinion of the early sections, including that on Caesar (*Encyclopaedia Metropolitana*, 10:550).

Caesar had three wives. His first wife, Cornelia, died, and his third, Calpurnia, outlived him. He was divorced only once— from his second wife, Pompeia, grandaughter of Sulla.

Dio several times alludes to Caesar's debauchery. In addition to Cleopatra, "he had his intrigues with ever so many other women—with all, doubtless, who chanced to come in his way . . ." (*Roman History*, bk. 42, sec. 34; Loeb, 4:167. See also bk. 44, sec. 7; Loeb, 4:319). (Cf. Dr. Arnold's opinion that Caesar was "excessively addicted to gross sensualities" and that, although a great general gifted with a wide range of intellectual interests, "the whole range of history can hardly furnish a picture of greater [moral] deformity"—*Encyclopaedia Metropolitana*, 10:277. Dr. Arnold was so fascinated by Caesar that he even dreamed of being one of his assassins.)

Literally, *Halt* is a support or (foot)hold, figuratively a stay or (moral) stability. This last, broadly rendered as (moral) steadiness, is what A. has in mind here. It is a word with a long history in A.'s works. (See *CPW*, 3:16; 5:271, 274, 281, 283; 9:28. It is akin to *"Fixity"* in a letter to "K," July 25, 1857, in *L*.) He took it from Goethe, as he several times acknowledged. (For example, see *N-Bs*, 490, where, in 1848, he translated *Halt* as "steadiness.") It is an extremely important concept for him, involving more than mere opposition to moral laxity. It is a quality that keeps one from the destructive consequences of wavering or fluctuating, which A. complains about so frequently. (See *CPW*, 1:13, and p. 23.)

[6]   "everything . . ." is perhaps meant to complete the sentence concerning Caesar's lack of *Halt*, at the same time that it suggests the moral "point of view" the drama was to present. *Halt* is to be the sine qua non. (In his lecture "On the Modern Element in Literature," A. emphasizes that the age's intellectual deliverers need an appropriate point of view for comprehending the modern spectacle [*CPW*, 1:20].)

The fact that A. speaks of "bourgeois and philister" makes explicit his long-standing conviction that Rome was a modern society much like his own (see commentary for 35r[1], p. 161). "Philister" is an early version of "philistine," not yet anglicized. The concern with moral steadiness as well as with "seeing things as they really are" points toward his analysis of Hebraism and Hellensim in *Culture and Anarchy*.

[7]   Wilhelm Karl August Drumann, *Geschichte Roms . . .* (3:749n), quotes Sallust, *Bellum Catilinae:* "De poena possum equidem dicere id, quod res habet, in luctu atque miseriis mortem aerumnarum requiem non cruciatum esse; eam cuncta mortalium mala dissolvere; ultra neque curae neque gaudio locum esse. Caes. bei Sallust. B.C.51." (". . . as to the punishment, we may say, what is indeed the truth, that in trouble and distress, death is a relief from suffering, and not a torment; that it puts an end to all human woes; and that, beyond it, there is no place either for sorrow or joy"—*Sallust*, trans. Watson, 59–60.) The English translator notes that "this Epicurean doctrine prevailed very

much at Rome in Caesar's time, and afterwards" (59–60n; cf. commentary on 13r[6], p. 73).

A.'s attention was probably drawn to Drumann by George Long's translation of Plutarch, *The Civil Wars of Rome,* which A. owned and admired (*CPW,* 3:136). Long's notes frequently refer to Drumann (as well as to Dion Cassius). A.'s notebooks indicate that he was reading "In Drumann" in September and October, 1855, suggesting that he was already familiar with the work. He turned to it again in September, 1856, for "Sulla, Caelius &c—" (*N-Bs,* 558 and 560).

Additional Works Cited

Classical writers have been omitted except when a specific edition or translation has been mentioned.

Allott, Kenneth. "A Background for 'Empedocles on Etna.' " *E & S,* n.s., 21 (1968): 80–100.

Arnold, Thomas. *Passages in a Wandering Life.* London: Arnold, 1900.

Barante, [A.-G.-P. B., baron] de. *Tableau de la littérature française pendant le dix-huitième siècle.* Paris, 1813.

———. *A Tableau of French Literature during the Eighteenth Century.* London, 1833.

Barbier, Auguste. *Iambes et poèmes.* Edited by Ch.-M. Garnier. Oxford, 1907.

———. *Satires et poèmes.* Paris, 1837.

The Bhagvat-Geeta. Translated by C. Wilkins. London, 1785.

Bonnerot, Louis. *Matthew Arnold, Poète: Essai de biographie psychologique.* Paris: Didier, 1947.

Bouillé, [F.-C.-A., marquis] de. *Mémoires sur la révolution française depuis son origine* . . . . 2 vols. in 1. Paris, 1801.

Bunsen, Christian Carl Josias. *Aegyptens Stelle in der Weltgeschichte.* 5 vols. Hamburg, 1845–57.

Burke, Edmund. *Correspondence.* Edited by Charles William, Earl Fitzwilliam, and Sir Richard Bourke. 4 vols. London, 1844.

Carlyle, Thomas. *The Works.* Edited by H. D. Traill. Centenary Edition. 30 vols. Boston: 1897–1901.

Christ, Carol. *The Finer Optic.* New Haven: Yale University Press, 1975.

Clough, Arthur Hugh. *The Correspondence.* Edited by Frederick L. Mulhauser. 2 vols. Oxford: Clarendon Press, 1957.

Cousin, V[ictor]. *Cours de l'histoire de la philosophie.* Paris, 1829.

———. *Cours de philosophie.* Paris, 1828.

———. *Course of the History of Modern Philosophy.* Translated by O. W. Wight. 2 vols. Edinburgh, 1852.

Curtius, Ernst. *The History of Greece.* Translated by A. W. Ward. 5 vols. London, 1868–73.

Davis, Arthur Kyle, Jr. *Matthew Arnold's Letters: A Descriptive Checklist.* Charlottesville: University Press of Virginia, 1968.

De Vere, Aubrey, *The Search after Proserpine. Recollections of Greece and Other Poems.* London, 1843.

————. *The Waldenses, or The Fall of Rora: a Lyrical Sketch. With Other Poems.* Oxford, 1842.

Dickens, Charles. *The Letters of Charles Dickens.* Edited by Madeline House, and Graham Storey, et al. Pilgrim Edition. 5 vols. to date. Oxford: Clarendon Press, 1965–.

Dickinson, Emily. *The Poems.* Edited by Thomas H. Johnson. 3 vols. Cambridge, Mass.: Harvard University Press, 1955.

Diels, Hermann, ed. *Die Fragmente der Vorsokratiker. Griechisch und deutsch.* Berlin, 1903.

Diogenes Laertius. *Lives of Eminent Philosophers.* Translated by R. D. Hicks. 2 vols. Loeb. London: Heinemann, 1925.

Dion Cassius [Cassius Dio Cocceianus]. *Dio's Roman History.* Translated by Ernest Cary. 9 vols. Loeb. London: Heinemann, 1914–27.

Dramas for the Stage, by George Stephens, Review of. *Spectator,* April 18, 1846, 377–78.

Drumann, W[ilhelm]. *Geschichte Roms in seinem Uebergange von der republikanischen zur monarchischen Verfassung. . . .* 6 vols. Koenigsberg, 1834–44.

Dunlop, John. *The History of Fiction.* 3d ed. London, 1845.

Dunn, Waldo Hilary. *James Anthony Froude: A Biography.* 2 vols. Oxford: Clarendon Press, 1961–63.

Eckermann, Johann Peter. *Conversations of Goethe with Eckermann.* Translated by John Oxenford. Everyman. London: Dent, 1930.

Emerson, R. W. *Essays.* [*First Series.*] Preface by Thomas Carlyle. London, 1841.

————. *Essays. Second Series.* London, 1844.

Encyclopaedia Metropolitana. 29 vols. London, [1817–45].

Epictetus. *The Discourses.* Translated by George Long. London, 1877.

Froude, J. A. *The Nemesis of Faith.* London, 1849.

Glanvill, Joseph. *The Vanity of Dogmatizing.* London, 1661.

Goethe, J. W. von. *Correspondence between Schiller and Goethe, from 1794 to 1805.* 2 vols. Translated by L. D. Schmitz. Bohn. London, 1877–79.

————. *Elective Affinities.* Translated by Elizabeth Mayer and Louise Bogan. Chicago: Regnery, 1963.

————. *Goethe's Autobiography.* Translated by R. O. Moon. Washington, D.C.: Public Affairs Press, 1949.

————. *Goethes Briefe an Frau von Stein aus den Jahren 1776 bis 1826.* Edited by Adolf Schöll. 3 vols. Weimar, 1848–51.

————. *Goethe's Color Theory.* Translated by Charles Eastlake. Edited by Rupprecht Matthaei. New York: Van Nostrand Reinhold, 1971.

Gomperz, Theodor. *Greek Thinkers.* Translated by Laurie Magnus. 4 vols. London: Murray, 1901–12.

Guizot, [François]. *Pourquoi la révolution d'Angleterre a-t-elle réussi? Discours sur l'histoire de la révolution d'Angleterre.* Paris, 1850.

————. *On the Causes of the Success of the English Revolution of 1640–1688.* [Translated by Mrs. Austin.] London, 1850.

————. *Why Was the English Revolution Successful? A Discourse on the History of the English Revolution.* Translated by William Hazlitt. 2d ed. London, 1850.

Heidegger, Martin. *Sein und Zeit.* Halle, 1927.

Heine, Heinrich. *Reisebilder.* 4 vols. Hamburg, 1826–31.

Houghton, R. E. C. "Letter of Matthew Arnold." *TLS,* May 19, 1932, 368.

Johnson, W. Stacy. *The Voices of Matthew Arnold.* New Haven: Yale University Press, 1961.

Karsten, Simon, ed. *Philosophorum Graecorum veterum, praesertim qui ante Platonem floruerunt, operum reliquiae.* 2 vols. Amsterdam, 1830–38.

Kermode, Frank. *The Sense of an Ending.* New York: Oxford University Press, 1967.

Larchey, Lorédan. *Dictionnaire des noms.* Paris, 1880.

Layard, Austen Henry. *Nineveh and Its Remains.* 2 vols. London, 1849.

Lewis, George Cornewall. *An Essay on the Influence of Authority in Matters of Opinion.* London, 1849.

Marlowe, Christopher. *The Works.* 3 vols. Pickering. London, 1826.

Maurice, Frederick, ed. *The Life of Frederick Denison Maurice.* 2 vols. London, 1884.

Michelet, Jules. *Histoire de France.* 17 vols. Paris, 1833–67.

Mill, J. S. *On Liberty.* London, 1859.

Miller, J. Hillis. *The Disappearance of God.* Cambridge, Mass.: Harvard University Press, 1963.

Montégut, Emile. "Les symptômes du temps, III." *RDM,* July 1, 1848, 106–19.

Musset, Alfred de. *La confession d'un enfant du siècle.* 2 vols. Paris, 1836.

"The Nimroud Sculptures." *Illustrated London News,* December 16, 1848, 373–74.

Nineveh and Its Remains, by Austen Henry Layard, Review of. *Times,* February 9, 1849, 5.

Pater, Walter. *The Works.* Library Edition. 10 vols. London: Macmillan, 1910.

Planche, Gustave. "Poètes et romanciers modernes de la France. XXV. M. Auguste Barbier. *Satires et Poèmes.*" *RDM,* July 1, 1837, 54–78.

Plato. *The Dialogues.* Translated by B. Jowett. 4th ed. 4 vols. Oxford: Clarendon Press, 1953.

Plutarch. *The Civil Wars of Rome: Select Lives.* Translated by George Long. 5 vols. London, 1844–48.

Porter, Robert Ker. *Travels in Georgia, Persia, Armenia, Ancient Bablylonia, &c. &c. during the Years 1817, 1818, 1819, and 1820.* 2 vols. London, 1821–22.

Rémusat, Charles de. *Passé et présent, mélanges.* 2 vols. Paris, 1847.

Sainte-Beuve, C. A. *Causeries de lundi.* 15 vols. Paris, 1851–62.

————. *Portraits contemporains.* 5 vols. Paris, 1882–88.

Saisset, Emile. "Giordano Bruno et la philosophie au seizième siècle." *RDM*, June 15, 1847, 1071–1105.

Sallust, Florus, and Velleius Paterculus. Translated by John Selby Watson. Bohn. London, 1852.

Sand, George. *Jacques.* 2 vols. Paris, 1834.

[Schindler, Anton Felix.] *The Life of Beethoven.* Edited by Ignace Moscheles. 2 vols. London, 1841.

Sells, Iris E. *Matthew Arnold and France.* 2d ed. New York: Octagon Press, 1970.

Shaw, Bernard. *The Bodley Head Bernard Shaw: Collected Plays with Their Prefaces.* 7 vols. London: Bodley Head, 1970–74.

Spinoza, Baruch. *Ethics.* [Translated by Andrew Boyle.] Everyman. London: Dent, 1910.

————. *Opera quotquot reperta sunt recognoverunt.* Edited by J. van Vloten and J. P. N. Land. 3d ed. 4 vols. The Hague: Nijhoff, 1914.

Stanley, Arthur Penrhyn. *The Life and Correspondence of Thomas Arnold, D.D.* 2 vols. London, 1844.

Stephens, George. *Dramas for the Stage.* 2 vols. London, 1846.

Stillingfleet, Edward. *Origines Sacrae, or a Rational Account of the Grounds of Christian Faith.* London, 1662.

[Taylor, Henry.] Review of *The Waldenses, or the Fall of Rora*, by Aubrey De Vere. *QR* 72 (1843): 142–65.

Tennyson, Alfred. *In Memoriam.* London, 1850.

Tinker, Chauncey Brewster. "Arnold's Poetic Plans." *YR* 22 (1933): 782–93.

Trilling, Lionel. *Matthew Arnold.* Rev. ed. New York: Meridian, 1955.

Ullmann, S. O. A. "Dating Through Calligraphy: The Example of 'Dover Beach.'" *SB* 26 (1973): 19–36.

Ward, Mrs. Humphry. *A Writer's Recollections.* London: Collins, 1918.

Index

Topic headings often include their opposites (e.g., cold-warm).